Quality Mentoring for Student Teachers:

A Principled Approach to Practice

Della Fish

David Fulton Publishers
London

David Fulton Publishers Ltd
2 Barbon Close, London WC1N 3JX

First published in Great Britain by
David Fulton Publishers 1995

Note: The right of Della Fish to be identified as the author of this work
has been asserted by her in accordance with the Copyright, Designs and
Patents Act 1988.

British Library Cataloguing in Publication Data

A catalogue record for this book is available from the British Library

ISBN 1-85346-351-1

Typeset by Action Typesetting Limited, Gloucester

Printed in Great Britain by BPC Books & Journals, Exeter

Contents

Acknowledgements

I acknowledge with gratitude the following people who provided me with help, support and personal education which resulted in the preparation of this publication. Many students, mentors in schools and field-work supervisors (or equivalent) in a range of caring professions have helped me, over a number of years, to refine my thinking and my practice. I am only sorry that it is impossible to name them all. Joan Bookham, vice-principal of Hereford College of Education first educated me systematically in classroom supervision in the late 1960s and laid the foundations for this work. Michael Golby introduced me to Curriculum Studies and has offered encouragement in the production of this publication. Sheila Twinn helped me to refine Strands of Reflection (see pp. 139–43). Evelyn Usher proof-read and corrected drafts with endless patience and good humour.

Any opinions expressed are entirely mine and are associated neither with the establishment that was called West London Institute (and is now a part of Brunel University) where I was a principal lecturer, nor with Exeter University, where I hold an appointment as honorary research fellow at the School of Education.

List of Abbreviations

BA/BSc/QTS	Bachelor of Arts/Bachelor of Science with qualified Teacher Status
BEd	Bachelor of Education
CATE	Committee for the Accreditation of Teacher Education
CNAA	Council for National Academic Awards
DES	Department of Education and Science
DFE	Department for Education
GNVQ	General National Vocational Qualification
HE	Higher Education
HEFCE	Higher Education Funding Council for England
HEI	Higher Education Institution
HMI	Her Majesty's Inspector
HMSO	Her Majesty's Stationery Office
INSET	In-service Education and Training of Teachers
IT	Information Technology
ITE	Initial Teacher Education
ITT	Initial Teacher Training
LEA	Local Education Authority
MOTE	Modes of Teacher Education
NC	National Curriculum
NFER	National Foundation for Educational Research
NQT	Newly Qualified Teacher
NVQ	National Vocational Qualification
OFSTED	Office for Standards in Education
OU	Open University
PA (model)	Professional Artistry (model)
PGCE	Postgraduate Certificate of Education
SCAA	Schools Curriculum and Assessment Authority

TES	*Times Educational Supplement*
TP	Teaching Practice
TR (model)	Technical Rational (model)
TTA	Teacher Training Agency

Special note

For clarity, the works of David Carr and Wilfred Carr are referred to in the body of the text using either their Christian names or initials in addition to their surname, as appropriate, and not simply their surname, since their subject matter and publication dates are similar.

Introduction

(i)

This book is addressed to both primary and secondary teachers who are preparing to undertake new mentoring roles in initial teacher education (ITE) under the government's new arrangements. It is written in the belief that mentoring by teachers in schools should always operate in partnership with tutors in higher education because this provides the best educational preparation for joining the teaching profession. The mentor, here, is defined broadly as *any* teacher who works in schools with student teachers to improve their practice. The concerns of this publication are with knowledge, understanding, capacities and skills that are common to such mentoring across all age-ranges.

The material presented here is different from that in previous books on mentoring in the following four respects:

1. It views the enterprise of learning to be a teacher as concerned with learning to be a member of the teaching profession rather than as learning to be a proficient classroom practitioner.

2. It therefore sees the intention of mentoring as educating students to become members of a profession rather than as training them to be deliverers of the National Curriculum to classes of pupils.

3. It seeks to prepare quality mentors by offering them education rather than training.

4. Its philosophy is that such mentor preparation, though ideally aimed from the start at whole-school level, is more likely in

practice to be taken up by individuals or at best by small groups within the school, thus developing school-wide expertise only incrementally.

What is offered here, therefore, is some means to work towards quality mentoring, based upon mentor *education*, rather than training. This involves offering a basis for both discussing some central issues and for trying out and considering mentoring practices. It does not mean providing a blueprint for good mentoring. As Alexander says of good practice, quality mentoring will be achieved 'dialectically and empirically, not by decree' (Alexander 1990, p.72). In order to provide a basis for these twin concerns about issues and practices, this book focusses on:

- the traditions and the present knowledge-base of ITE

- the complex character of classroom practice and its social traditions

- the nature of the wider professional perspectives characteristic of a member of the teaching profession

- techniques of investigation and reflection which enable professionals to refine classroom practice and professional activity.

In doing so it offers:

- experience of what is involved in learning through practice, ways of enabling students to learn through practice, and analysis of such experience

- consideration of the strengths and weaknesses of various activities associated with observation, debriefing, assessment

- experience in articulating and considering ethically the personal theory that underlies professional action, and of enabling students to do so

- experience in uncovering, scrutinising and thinking ethically about the principles and grounds of professional action, and of providing support for students doing so.

It invites response from the reader throughout by offering during each chapter a series of points to consider and tasks to work on, either alone or with a colleague.

This work is directed at the individual mentor (teacher who works with students in school) but it might also be used by a school as a basis for school-based in-service sessions. It draws upon the extensive knowledge-base of initial teacher education, its research and traditions, especially as developed in recent decades. It is based upon school-based whole-school mentor preparation courses, offered in both primary and secondary schools and directed by the author, as well as the developing literature on mentoring. It represents the fruits of reflections upon twenty years of working with both primary and secondary students in the classroom and school. It is grounded in extensive work with teachers, tutors and students in the school classroom (see Fish 1989), and in on-going practitioner research on mentoring courses.

This book is written in the belief that clarification of one's uncertainties about teaching and learning and a willingness to investigate, reflect upon and refine one's theories and practices provide a better base from which to work with student teachers than the unfounded and quickly punctured certainty that springs from ignorance of the complexities. It is addressed to those who seek rather than to those who know. In offering an educational foundation for mentoring it challenges the skills-based training approach of many current mentoring guides.

Its intentions are to enable readers to:

- recognise the problematic nature of teaching and learning in schools and in ITE

- have an open mind about their own practice and theories

- become experienced in reflecting on their own practice

- know how to continue to investigate and refine practice and theory

- be able to articulate their personal philosophical approach to teaching and mentoring

- be ready to enable students to articulate their own personal approach to teaching and to find their own ways of operating successfully in a classroom

- form a clear idea of how they want to operate as mentors in the classroom and the school as a whole

- know how their mentoring relates to work done with students in higher education (HE).

In short, this book is directed at setting the feet of mentors on a path towards a principled approach to practice, built upon the twin foundations of seeking better understanding of issues and continual refinement of practice which is based upon sound principles, and having, as a central characteristic, a view of quality which rests upon professional insight (evidenced by wise practice and sound professional judgements), rather than on measuring required visible behaviour.

(ii)

The rationale for the book springs from comparing two broad views about teaching and learning to teach.

One view, **the technical rational** (TR) **view**, is that teaching is a simple set of competences and that these can be learnt by the student practising and the mentor advising and assessing. Here the mentor needs to learn skills and strategies of counselling, observing and assessing of the kind most frequently found in mentor training courses. It is assumed that, having done so, the mentor will merely have to apply them in practice in order to train the student to deliver the National Curriculum. The skills and strategies enshrined in the TR view are relatively simple to learn (though the professional judgement about when and how to operate them is more difficult than its proponents admit). This approach certainly offers one starting point for mentors in times of limited resources, but some people have reservations about its educational qualities and its longer term advantages.

The other view, **the reflective practitioner view**, is that teaching is a complex, dynamic, social activity with a moral dimension. It is embedded in important sets of traditions and theoretical perspectives. In this case, helping the student to learn practice involves the mentor in:

- acknowledging and trying to understand this complexity

- seeking to articulate, and keep under review, a clear principled base to personal practice (and recognising that practice itself can often fall short of this)

- knowing how research on teaching and learning can enlighten practice

- knowing how to investigate practice, how to unearth the theory from it and how to reflect upon it, theorise about it and challenge it with formal theory

- understanding how individual practice relates to the moral and the traditional aspects of professional practice and recognising the implications of this for teaching

- being able to draw out of a student the ideas, beliefs, assumptions and values that lie at the base of that student's practice

- being able to help the student to find new approaches to practice and their rationales

- being able to help the student find his/her own preferred approach to professional practice

- being able to engage in discussions with the student about the purposes of education, in order to enable the student to explore how his/her own practice relates to the moral and social traditions of teaching.

The reflective practitioner view of enabling students to learn to teach is more demanding than the TR approach. It requires a greater degree of intellectual and professional time and energy and a willingness to work at articulating the professional knowledge which teachers traditionally draw upon in practice but often find hard to put into words. That is, it requires more of teachers than simply allowing students into their classroom and demonstrating successful teaching in front of them. Further, it takes more effort and greater resources to prepare such mentors. But it offers student and mentor a learning adventure in which each can contribute to the growth of the other in an infinite variety of ways.

It would seem from an analysis of Department for Education (DFE) documents on quality control in ITE under new partnership arrangements (including guidelines for inspecting partnership schools) that they see the TR approach to ITE as likely to gain partner schools a 'satisfactory' rating from the Office for Standards in Education (OFSTED), but regard a successful reflective practitioner approach as likely to lead to a 'good' or 'very good' report. Both approaches to mentoring will be offered as a means of exploring key issues in each chapter of the first two parts of this book.

(iii)

The book is offered in three parts. The first part deals with a range of issues that all mentors need to appreciate if their work is to be of high quality. These are:

- contextual issues for mentoring (an understanding of the scope and aims of ITE; how it developed historically and why it is as it is today)

- the complexities of defining professionalism and two key models of professionalism that influence ITE courses today, and how these cash out into models of teacher education

- how students learn practice and theory and how they can be helped to do so

- the broad processes and responsibilities of mentoring according to government documents.

For each issue a range of differing approaches and views is considered, some practical investigations are offered for teachers to carry out alone or with a colleague (other teacher or student) and some further reading is recommended.

The second part focusses specifically on mentoring in the classroom and how to enable students to become not only proficient teachers but also professional teachers who understand the deeper issues that influence their practice, who know how to investigate their practice and who are able to develop and refine their practice. This section begins with a chapter on notions of good practice – which are central to views on how to develop and assess the work of student teachers. Later chapters focus on observing, debriefing and assessing the student. For each aspect a range of differing approaches and views is considered, some practical investigations are offered for teachers to carry out alone or with a colleague (other teacher or student), the role of HE is considered and some further reading is recommended as follow-up.

The third part considers the important wider role of the mentor which is often neglected or treated very briefly in other mentoring books. This section looks at how the mentor can help the student towards becoming a member of the teaching profession rather than simply becoming a proficient performer in an individual classroom. This involves supporting the student in his/her investigations of whole-school issues and explorations of some practical school-based manifestations of deeper professional matters. It also involves understanding the whole-course approach to teacher preparation and the role of college-based work and of the HE tutor.

Accordingly the chapters consider whole-school and profession-wide issues; designing an ITE course to enable the student to learn to be a professional; the implications for the whole-school of its partnership in ITE; and the indicators of quality partnership between schools and HE.

(iv)

Postscript

This book is about quality mentoring as opposed to mentor training. To ignore the first and last parts of this book would be to ignore the very issues that distinguish the quality mentor from the trained mentor. Readers are therefore advised not simply to skip to the practical chapters but to read the text in chronological order.

Della Fish
September 1994

Part 1

Quality Mentoring:
Understanding the Enterprise

CHAPTER 1

Mentoring: Some Major Contextual Issues

Introduction

Under the new government arrangements for ITE, teachers working with student teachers in school will be acting as mentors. Being a mentor is specifically different from previous responsibilities and modes of operation as a teacher supervisor or a class teacher receiving a student for teaching practice. It now involves taking on the entire role of educating the student to be a teacher. Even where there is still a tutor visiting the school regularly, that tutor's role will now be different. Teachers will be in the forefront of working with the student. Working with adult students towards a professional qualification (being the gatekeeper of a profession) is quite different from teaching young pupils the National Curriculum. Working as part of ITE is to be open to scrutiny by students, the college providers who have some responsibility for quality control, and OFSTED who will inspect schools' provision for students whenever they inspect teacher training in an individual HEI. The differences between this and previous experiences of having a student are awesome. It also means knowing about ITE in much more detail.

ITE is an enterprise characterised by its own areas of empirical knowledge, traditions, ways of operating, major research bases as well as government regulations. All of these are permeated by conflicting stances (shaped by conflicting values) towards teaching, learning, theory, practice and research. Teacher education (like all educational enterprises) is inevitably a field of problematic issues and essentially contested agendas. It is not so much that these need to be maintained under the new arrangements as that they need to be known about, recognised and reviewed by anyone working centrally in the field in order to be able to debate them with students (as part of students' entitlement to education) and to be able to refine, develop, change or otherwise improve practice in ITE for the future.

This Introduction seeks to highlight some of the major contextual issues for mentoring by offering, in four sections, four important perspectives, each of which focusses down progressively upon the responsibilities of mentors and which, taken together, show how the new mentoring role for teachers has evolved. These perspectives are: (i) a consideration of the intentions of ITE; (ii) a broad historical context showing the evolution of ITE; (iii) a focus on the last years of the twentieth century, showing how the teacher has come to replace the tutor in ITE; and (iv) some basic information about what the government now requires of mentors working in ITE. Through this approach, this Introduction presents an overview of some essentially problematic issues of ITE. In doing so it raises and tries to clarify some of the matters that students themselves may wish to discuss in detail with teacher-mentors, just as they once would have discussed them with college tutors. Some of the key questions it addresses are as follows:

- What are (and what should be) the main intentions of ITE and what might be left to in-service work?

- How has ITE come to be where it is now? (What can we learn from its history?)

- What are the government requirements of teachers, students and tutors?

- What roles are envisaged for school and college?

- What values are enshrined in the key government documents?

- What are the essential differences between being a supervisor and being a mentor?

(i)

Intentions and ITE

Aims and education

At an early point in educational preparation for a profession, as well as at subsequent stages towards qualification, issues about the aims of education and the aims of the profession will arise – even *should* arise. The mentor will need to be able to engage with these in order to enable students to explore them as they seek to establish their own philosophical base for professional practice. The following is an attempt to offer some purchase on the arguments.

Given that education is itself a value-based concept whose definition will depend upon whatever is most valued from a subjective range of possible and competing priorities, it is clear that any statement of aims will depend upon the values and experiences of those expressing them. Only the most general of aims are likely to receive broad assent. Thus a clear set of values (in fact a whole political ideology) is at work behind the National Curriculum. It is to be seen not least in the valuing, by those who set it up, of some subjects over others and of a false consensus about what should be taught and how. Clear signals about the values of those in power are also evident in the imposition upon professional experts of ways of operating which have been created by those outside the profession (though this is not to deny the rights of all of the stakeholders in education to have a say). In making such statements a further set of values (my own) is being revealed.

The imposed consensus about the National Curriculum makes it seem that there are simple and universally agreed answers to the question of what should be taught in schools. Superficially it could be argued (and government documents certainly imply) that since decisions about what to teach have already been made and are law, teachers must now be trained to work within these, and to deliver the National Curriculum without needing to consider the ends (goals/intentions) of education. But this is to ignore the essential relationship between means and ends. Student teachers need to come to grips with the problematic nature of aims so that they can begin to recognise and consider their own views and values in order to make professional decisions about those actions which are still under (and will always be under) their control. Further, arguably, if they are to be full professionals, they need to be aware of and contribute to debates about means and ends, since such debates should not be conducted, and such judgements should not be made, only by those outside the profession.

Addressing means and ends quickly raises deep moral issues. (For example: How should professionals/teachers/learners be treated? Who is entitled to what in the distribution of educational goods?

What is education for? What are schools for? On what principles should children be assessed, how do various assessment tools view pupils as human beings, and on what bases should student teachers be admitted to or prevented from joining the profession?) Is it not the place of ITE to consider such issues? What ought to be and what are the aims of ITE?

Aims and teacher education

The following questions, about the aims for and the nature of teacher education illustrate something of the complexity of these issues. As we shall see in detail in this and later chapters, these questions are not the prelude to idle philosophising. The ways in which politicians and educators have sought to answer them have given rise to the practical arrangement we have for ITE today. Understanding this helps us to explain past practice, to think analytically about present government initiatives and may even help us to clarify the range of hopes for the future.

TASK 1.1: PREPARATION FOR REFLECTION

Alone or with a colleague
1.   Offer your own answers to the questions in the main text below.

2.   Explore your replies to see what values and priorities lie underneath them.

3.   Consider your own professional philosophies.

4.   If possible share your findings with a colleague.

Preliminary comment
We do not always know what it is we personally value until we come up against such questions. On considering our responses we may well be shocked that there are conflicts between what we say and what we do, or even between our preferred answer to one question compared with that to another.

But at least to recognise these inconsistencies is:
—   to have unearthed matters that will repay further exploration

—   to know more about how we wish to respond to questions about educational aims

— to have the power to challenge, refine, develop or change our ideas

— to begin to develop or to refine continuously our own overall teaching philosophy

— to be able to discuss these ideas in an informed way with students.

● Arguably, one of the tasks of ITE is to enable student teachers to begin to explore their values and to develop their own philosophy of education/teaching/professionalism.

● Equally it is important that those working with students do not consider that they *know* and have *'cracked'* these things. Certainty about such matters arises only from ignorance about their complexity, and is a sure way of stopping student learning dead in its tracks.

● You may wish to return to and revise your responses to the questions in the light of later discussions in this book.

Some questions about teacher education

1. What do new teachers need to know? Should ITE aim to equip students with only that which is necessary to deliver the National Curriculum to a particular class (to be an efficient class teacher) or should it also educate them about their wider role as a teacher in schools and in a profession?

2. What ought to be involved in learning to be an efficient classroom teacher? How might this be learnt?

3. What is the relationship between what students know and how they teach?

4. What is, or might be, involved in the wider role of the teacher, what is involved in coming to be a full member of a profession, and how can students acquire professional knowledge?

5. Is it legitimate to describe the less ambitious set of aims in Question 1 above as Initial Teacher Training (ITT) and the wider focussed set of aims referred to in Question 4 as ITE?

6. How important is it to maintain the professional nature of teaching and to be a member of a profession today? (Has the importance of professionalism been eroded by changes in

views about authority and accountability? Has the meaning of the word 'professional' changed?)

7. How important is it that teaching is an all-graduate profession? How important is it that teachers should undergo a rigorous course of ITE which leads to a validated HE qualification?

8. What should be attempted in the short-term in ITE and what should be left to the longer term (in-service work)? Should ITE seek to spend time only on learning the basic classroom survival skills (leaving more sophisticated matters to in-service work)?

9. How important is it that the teaching profession should play a significant part in defining entry standards, assessing students and evaluating ITE courses?

10. How far can and should a course of professional education be prescribed from outside the profession? Who has a legitimate voice in, and who should decide, the aims and the content of teacher education?

11. What exactly is/should be HE's contribution to ITE? What place does a university have in the vocational and professional preparation of teachers?

As we have already seen, there are no simple, universal answers to these questions. All responses are shaped by our values and our depth of understanding. But a particular response to them from outside the profession is currently shaping ITE. Further questions arise, therefore, about how this has come to happen and what action is required of mentors and tutors. Again, the following offers a framework which those anxious to provide quality mentoring will need to be aware of in order to make sense of their own place in both history and the present.

(ii)

The evolution of ITE: a broad historical context

This is not the place to provide extensive detail about the history of ITE; it is written about at length elsewhere (Edwards 1992a,

1992b and 1994; my own earlier summary, Fish 1989; Gardner 1993; Reid 1985; Wilkin 1990). However, it is worth noting some of the major issues that have affected the preparation of teachers, and to observe their patterns of occurrence and re-emergence during the nineteenth and twentieth centuries. An overview of the last twenty years in respect of the developments towards present partnership arrangements is also instructive. Readers will note the echoing in these historical accounts of issues already raised in the previous section. These matters are highly relevant for mentors and students, and strikingly link past and present. As Bernbaum said, ITE:

> is currently the subject of much speculation and apparent innovation and change. This was also the case in the 1880s where the origins of the present system of training graduate teachers are to be found.
> (Bernbaum 1985, p.7)

Further, the wider perspectives of two centuries of upheaval offer something of a sense of inevitability derived from *déjà vu*, since, as Stones notes: 'many current "innovations" are merely re-runs of nineteenth century practice' (Stones 1992a, p.219).

Some of the most significant trends which emerge from a review of the nineteenth- and twentieth-century history of teacher preparation are:

1. the swings backwards and forwards across the two centuries between school-based and focussed, and college-based and focussed, teacher preparation (and the associated swings of status for theory and practice)

2. the swings between teachers being seen as agents of church and state (the key governing authorities) or as potential *agents provocateurs*

3. the associated swings between teachers being offered a narrow apprenticeship training and a wider professional education

4. differences in approach to teacher preparation by colleges and universities.

To some extent, of course, these are interlinked issues, selected for their significance from a wider range of such issues, and unable to be accorded full justice here. But the flavour of the historical context can be offered.

1.   The swings between school- and college-focussed ITE

It seems clear from the history of education of the nineteenth and twentieth centuries that ITT has swung slowly backwards and forwards between the essentially college-based, academic and theoretical, and the essentially school-based and practical. (See Gardner 1993 for a very full account of this.) Gardner reminds us that at the formal start of teacher preparation at the beginning of the nineteenth century, training was typically based not in colleges but in schools, and embraced the 'innovatory and voguish monitorial principles associated with Lancaster and Bell'. This training was offered to those who came to learn a mechanical system and pick up tips. Under the Kay-Shuttleworth pupil-teacher scheme, introduced in 1846, there was to be a balance between learning mechanical skills and gaining a personal moral education, but in fact the practical skills were emphasised. It was the 1870 Education Act which, providing as it did for compulsory elementary education for all, inevitably caused pressures on the quality and quantity of trained teachers. The pendulum thus began its swing back towards emphasising the role of the college. Broadly, training was based in the schools until nearly the end of the nineteenth century, but by the end of the 1920s it had become firmly rooted in the colleges. In the intervening thirty years the tensions of transition and change, as Gardner points out 'in some respects mirrors that of our own age' (Gardner 1993, p.22).

During these years the narrowness of craft skills was beginning to be seen as a problem, and this led to the demand for more theoretical work. By 1944, with the advent of secondary education for all, there was further pressure for the academic preparation of teachers. Evidence of the extreme college-focussed approach to teacher preparation is found in the 1960s and 1970s characterised by strong moves to establish the academic foundations of teaching and develop an all-graduate profession, by accentuating the college/university role and emphasising theory. And again, by contrast, the 1980s and early 1990s show government control of an extensive kind, directed at narrowing the training and returning it to schools (Gardner 1993, pp.28–30). Gardner sharpens the current relevance of all this by making the grim point that:

> in the critical decades of change at the close of the nineteenth century and the opening of the twentieth, the reforming pendulum was beginning its long swing from school to training institution. As it did so, it swept past the moment of partnership. A century later,

with the pendulum moving in the other direction, it would be well to bear this in mind.
(Gardner 1993, p.34)

The historical record, then, puts what we are experiencing today into perspective. But, were this better known and the lessons of the past acknowledged, would there really be more chance of arresting the pendulum at full partnership as Gardner implies? It seems unlikely because of the other, related issues – not least the following one.

2. *Teachers: agents of the state or* agents provocateurs?

Hopkins and Reid noted in 1985 that teacher education is vulnerable to the whims of politicians and bureaucrats. The history of two centuries seems to show that the controlling authorities (church and state) have often swung between seeing teachers as helpful servants and agents on the one hand and regarding their emancipation via their training on the other with fear and a determination to prevent it. Gardner notes that church and state sought to ensure that teachers acted as their agents:

> This was a central purpose behind the state's entry into the sponsorship and certification of teacher training in 1846. From that moment, effective forms of training, together with regular inspection by the recently-formed HMI, were envisaged not simply as mechanisms to improve the quality of schooling, but also to regulate and direct the daily activity of the teacher in the classroom. Since 1846, this is a capacity which the state has utilised in varying degrees according to perceived need and which it has never relinquished.
> (Gardner 1993, p.23)

The long and still unsuccessful campaign to establish a professional body for teaching is yet further testimony to this.

3. *Swings between apprenticeship training and professional education*

It takes little imagination to see that a simple device for limiting the emancipation offered to teachers by a wide education is to reduce their preparation to a narrow apprenticeship model in which practical skills are imparted, efficiency in learned strategies is emphasised and quality is defined in mechanical terms, but where debates about the wider and more complex issues are put out of bounds. Such moves have occurred at regular intervals during both centuries and are recorded, amongst others by Hopkins and Reid (1985) and Gardner (1993).

The changing language in which teacher preparation is described is symptomatic of such changes in thinking and attitudes. In the 1960s there were teacher training colleges; in the 1970s the same establishments were colleges of education. Interestingly, in the 1980s colleges of education were given wider educational perspectives. Almost all of them were changed from monotechnic institutions to polytechnics and institutes of higher education where a multiplicity of subjects was studied, and professional preparation of teachers began to be joined by that of health- and community-related professions. Now, in the 1990s, these same establishments are almost all universities but teacher preparation, though *validated* by universities, looks set to become the almost exclusive province of schools.

It seems that none of these changes were really about improvements in teacher education. They were responses to political agendas and financial constraints.

4. Differences in approach to teacher preparation by colleges and universities

In a previous publication (Fish 1989), I offered examples of the differences over the last twenty years between the training colleges' and polytechnics' approaches to ITE (validated by the Council for National Academic Awards (CNAA)) and that found in the universities. I attributed the powerful and (as I see it) misguided influence of some university voices on government policy (for example, those of Hirst, Hargreaves and O'Hear) to the fact that they were familiar with *only* university attitudes to teaching-practice and to teachers' roles in ITE. I argued that this caused them to cast the whole of ITE in a light true of only one half of the system.

The deep differences between the university system of teacher preparation and that of the colleges were endemic from the start. The training colleges emphasised craft expertise, established a desirable distance 'between teachers and their working-class parents and pupils', and produced students 'stuffed with useless facts and full of airs and graces' (Gardner 1993, p.27); they also kept them from forming any relationship with the different professional world of secondary (graduate) teachers. However, in time these colleges developed much closer and more genuine working links with schools than most of the university departments had.

By the end of the 1960s, as my own work in the colleges at this time shows (Fish 1989), there were many unsung and unacknowledged practical experiments involving tutors working in classes with students and teachers. Teaching practice was a serious enterprise and again involved both teacher and tutor. But, although the colleges were under the direction of Area Training Organisations (based at universities), the developments in the colleges in no way influenced the universities. The colleges lacked the research ethos of the universities and so these innovations went largely unrecorded. In contrast, university teacher training was still cast in a traditional mould (evident in my own postgraduate certificate of education (PGCE) training in the mid-1960s) which involved the odd 'administrative' visit by a tutor to a school, but little other contact between schools and the university.

These differences between the colleges and the universities, in respect of their attitudes to and the practices in schools, were accentuated in the 1970s and 1980s. The universities could no longer afford to maintain the validation and overall administration of college courses and the assessment of students, and the powerful influence of the CNAA came to be exercised over the colleges and polytechnics. Validation of courses (and tutors' jobs) came to depend upon the closer involvement of teachers in the planning, administration, delivery and evaluation of courses. Quite simply, courses were not validated by the CNAA unless the basic principles of involving teachers at all levels were adhered to. This enforced involvement of a few 'representative' teachers, though it did not amount to partnership, was far in advance of the less demanding method of considering courses adopted by most university senates, where the involvement of teachers was never a consideration.

Again, then, the two systems moved further apart – so much so that those who spoke for ITT from the university sector did not, on the whole, even seem to be aware of the CNAA system. Therefore, the complaints about the distance of teacher-training establishments from the real world of schools were relevant to only one side of the system, but were treated as if they applied to both. This gave the government the excuse to make changes that were no doubt planned – and for far from educational reasons.

It should be made clear, however, that the two systems described above do not represent a simple division between training for the

Bachelor of Education (BEd) on the one hand and the PGCE on the other, nor indeed training for primary versus secondary teaching. Although the teacher preparation system began by making distinctions between teachers for elementary and for secondary education, by the 1970s all the training providers were offering all of the four possible routes (BEd primary and secondary and PGCE primary and secondary). But within each of these particular routes, there was a multiplicity of different course experiences, and even within one establishment the character of the course changed over quite short periods of time (though it was always the case that the postgraduate (PGCE) courses were of one year's duration while the BEds were usually three- or four-year courses). Assumptions that each institution had its own distinctive character, and that those who gained one of the four main kinds of teaching qualifications share a set of experiences, knowledge, values and attitudes, may thus be quite erroneous.

TASK 1.2: POINTS FOR REFLECTION

Alone or with a colleague
Write down a personal account of your ITT. Add comments about any advanced long courses that have affected your teaching in the classroom. (NB *writing* it down is important for gaining maximum effect for later tasks.)

Then consider the following:

● How do your personal experiences relate to the context offered above?

● Examine your own written words for the origins of your own views on teacher preparation and the current system, and for your own values as they relate to the preparation of teachers.

● Share these with someone else, and compare and contrast your own and their actual experience of ITE and the emerging values.

(We all *assume* that everyone else has had the same experience and shares the same values – especially if we work together in the same school, or have the same college or the same qualification. The interest lies in the differences between us.)

(iii)

Replacing tutor with teacher: a focus on the last years of the twentieth century

An unequal partnership in ITE between schools and HEIs (with teachers taking the lead) is now a government requirement for the last years of the twentieth century. I believe that this idea has emerged during the 1980s and 1990s as a result of careful government orchestration, and for reasons far from educational. How this has been achieved is of importance to mentors since it reveals how their new responsibilities have come to be determined. Further, since partners are required to negotiate their own terms of partnership, it is important to be aware of the range of possibilities for organising partnerships and to know what is no longer acceptable.

The moves back to the school-based, classroom-focussed and essentially technical-practical approaches to ITE of the present decade have been a long time coming. They are recorded in detail in Wilkin (1990), who characterises partnership as a version of theory/practice relationship re-formulated in more practical terms, and in my own previous work (Fish 1989).

At least since 1944 (the McNair Report) there have been explicit and very clear calls for teachers to have more responsibility for student teachers in school. Wilkin claims that:

> the relationship between training institutions and schools has evolved over the last two or three decades from one of distant wariness and expediency to one of mutual co-operation and respect.
> (Wilkin 1990, p.4)

She argues that until the 1980s the incidence of *active* partnership was very limited (Wilkin 1990, p.12). She does, however, acknowledge that 'the public sector institutions were rather more advanced' in respect of involving teachers in supervision of students (Wilkin 1992b, p.82). I believe − as evidenced above − that all sorts of unrecorded but substantial investigations were made into partnership from the early 1970s onwards (though the term partnership is certainly a more recent conceptualisation of these moves).

The broad developments, however, have ranged from a voluntary involvement of teacher trainers in schools, initiated by the HEI, as part of an institution's course development, to an absolute requirement of full but teacher-led partnership as part of a fixed initial training curriculum. These changes have been introduced via a series of government circulars which all those engaged in the ITE enterprise need to know in some detail.

I have traced elsewhere (Fish 1989, pp.34–9) the postwar moves towards partnership and have shown how in the late 1970s in response to the Ruskin Speech a strong sense of the inadequacies of schools emerged through two major reports on schools in England (*Primary education in England* (1978) and *Aspects of secondary education* (1979).) The findings in the reports by implication concerned *all* schools (although both reports were selected surveys), and, by association therefore, teacher training. I have also detailed the increasingly prescriptive and converging tone of the key documents on initial training which emerged in the first half of the 1980s from the Department of Education and Science (DES) and Her Majesty's Inspectors (HMI).

I now see this period from 1981 to 1986 as the more tentative of two phases in a politically – that is ideologically – motivated strategy to nullify the role of HE in the preparation of teachers. The second phase, from 1988 to 1994, saw this strategy becoming far more overt and increasingly determined, as a result, presumably, of the return to office of the Tory government. Both of these phases are illuminating for those who would take centre stage in the ITE enterprise in the second half of this last decade of the millennium, since arguably they reveal that the government's interest is not actually in the education of student teachers, but in saving money and restricting the power and influence of the educational establishment by narrow, doctrinaire and quite undemocratic means.

Phase 1 (1981–1986): The move towards school-based ITE

The key documents of this period consisted of three HMI discussion papers (each one becoming less discursive and more prescriptive), a White Paper on teaching quality (designed to refocus the management of the teaching profession) and two DES circulars (designed to spell out the implications of government policy). All of these make detailed reference to school/college partnership in ITE. Their tone and content seemed, if increasingly irascible at least initially, to be the result of genuine concern to improve ITE. For example, *Teacher training in the secondary school: the implications of the HMI survey* (January 1981) contained an exhortation to link practice with theory and to extend school/college links, although it betrayed (an inaccurate) assumption that students received formal lectures (about theory) in college. The word 'opportunities' occurred frequently and the tone was not prescriptive (see Fish 1989).

By 1983, however, the tone had changed. *Teaching in schools: the content of initial training* contains the declamatory sentences and other forms of rhetoric which were later to become characteristic of most government statements about schools and about ITE. In a tone that brooks no argument it talks of the 'professional skills which initial training can give to an intending teacher' — the word 'give' showing a simplistic view of a course of professional preparation (DES 1983, p.10). It sees the acquisition of skills as the central and major content of teacher training, and again makes an inaccurate assumption that the relationship between college theory and school practice is that the theory precedes the practice. Using the ideas of Paul Hirst from a report which was published in 1979 and which was specifically about the *universities'* PGCE (secondary) training, the document *Teaching in schools* demands closer collaboration between schools and colleges, that tutors and teachers teach 'in each other's institutions' and experiment 'with carefully considered schedules of assessment for practical teaching'. It then speaks testily of the fact that:

> recommendations of this kind have been made for many years, and some institutions follow the practices discussed. If a true partnership is to be effected with the teaching profession, such examples of good practice should extend to all initial training courses.
> (DES 1983, p.11)

Within three months of this publication's appearance the government White Paper, *Teaching quality,* was published. It contained the then startling information that the Secretary of State for Education was to exercise arbitrary new powers to establish the Committee for the Accreditation of Teacher Education (CATE), in both a local and national form, through which he would grant approval (accreditation) for courses — only when they conformed to his requirements. Such courses would involve active partnership and would be taught by college tutors who had gained the now famous 'recent and relevant' teaching experience in schools. These became the first quality indicators in a teacher preparation course. Under the guise of calling for improved quality in teaching, then, the government had created the machinery for taking control of these matters. (And it was already clear that from now on the position of any Secretary of State for Education under a Tory government was going to become ever more powerful. Having invented one new set of powers unopposed, she/he was always going to be able to invent any others necessary to take total control of teacher education nationally. And so it has proved, and is still proving.)

Fifteen months after the publication of *Teaching quality, Circular 3/84* (DES 1984) appeared. It has since proved to be the first of many circulars which have increasingly narrowed down, simplified and (as many would argue) distorted the task of ITT. Together with explicatory Catenotes from the newly established CATE, it took control of the detail of initial training, reinforced the White Paper's comments and set up, in the form of seventeen criteria which courses had to fulfil, a series of hurdles to be cleared by all institutions seeking to offer teacher training. This enforced the revalidation of all courses. Four of these seventeen criteria concerned the formation of links and close working partnerships with a variety of schools. They required: the sharing of responsibility for planning, supervision and support of students in schools with experienced teachers, and the influential involvement of teachers in the assessment of students' practical performance (Criterion 3); that tutors should have recent and relevant experience (Criterion 4); that substantial parts of the course should be based in schools (Criterion 5); and the separation of the academic and practical assessment to ensure that students must pass the practical element (Criterion 6) (DES 1984, pp.6–7). The phrase 'adequate mastery of basic professional skills' appears also (DES 1984, p.8). Whoever drafted this knew little of the intricacies of initial training.

Indeed, as I pointed out at the time (Fish 1989, p.44), these requirements were based on at least four false assumptions:

- that teachers would have the motivation, the ability, the time and the resources needed to follow through these requirements

- that the skills, knowledge, capacities and abilities required for teaching children were either the same as, or so similar to, those needed for working with student teachers that no training or support would be necessary for teachers in their new role

- that experience of teaching is all that tutors need to bring to their college work

- that extending the length of practice is automatically going to improve the quality of that practice.

All of this was further reinforced in 1986 by *Catenote 4, Links between initial training institutions and schools*. It looked to a common 'spirit of partnership through which both trainers and teachers [could] make their own contributions towards a shared professional objective' (CATE 1986, p.7). It focussed on the organisation, management and assessment of students' teaching practice and school experience; the involvement of practising teachers in the selection and training of those students; and tutors' demonstration and reinforcement of their own teaching effectiveness in schools. It also talked about students developing and testing the practical classroom skills that they had (already) learnt in college. Here it can be seen that the mistaken notions about how courses actually operated persist. In fact, even in the early 1980s there was (at least in the non-university sector) a much closer integration of theory and practice than the Catenote implies. What the Catenote did not do, of course, was enable the provision of extra resources to help the development of these partnerships. As a result, its actual effect was to demand impractical changes which could never become deep-rooted and which the government could shortly claim had not been implemented. This then provided the basis for an even more dictatorial phase.

Phase 2 (1988–1994): The dismantling of the educational establishment

By 1988, then, a new approach to teaching and teacher training was discernible. Teachers were being strait-jacketed by the National Curriculum and by the new Teachers' Pay and Conditions. New routes to teaching were being devised to undercut the power of the training institutions. All official documents now used the term ITT rather than ITE.

The first licensed teachers' scheme was announced in 1988 with the appearance of a consultation document (DES 1988). The scheme placed the licensee immediately in the schools under licence for two years. This meant 'learning on the job', and in that sense fitted the emerging trend to move ITE to job training in the work-place. In other words it explicitly cut out the contribution of HE, unless the employer chose to make the licensee attend an HE course. Decisions about training were placed entirely in the hands of the employers who would require only that which they deemed appropriate.

The whole approach and language of the document that introduced the scheme come from the world of business. It is about cost-effective apprenticeship. This fits with the government's concern only with the short-term. In the long term the 'trained' licensee would have limited transferability and limited means to extend, develop and refine practice. In a stroke teaching had been deprived of its professional status. Further, this scheme introduced the notion of mentors and mentoring to teacher training, and did a disservice to that concept, because the pressures on the scheme caused a utilitarian and training character to be attached to this role. (Apprenticeship versions of initial training lead naturally to apprenticeship versions of mentor training.) Originally little or no training was offered. When it was eventually offered, it was brief, and concerned with very basic issues.

This move, which was clearly aimed at breaking the power of HE over teacher education, was very closely followed by the publication of *Circular 24/89* (DES 1989). This circular transferred control over the ITE curriculum and content from the colleges to the political arena, and gave the upper hand and the maximum exposure to teachers. (Tutors were barely mentioned and when they were it was in derogatory terms.) Teachers were now to be involved in planning courses and in their evaluation. Local CATE committees which, under *Circular 3/84*, had been bodies consisting of course leaders and their associated teachers, which encouraged and promoted useful links between colleges and schools, and which were centred on individual HEI, now became bodies run across local groups of (competing) institutions. Local democracy thus became less meaningful since the local CATE committee was reduced to a bureaucratic tool. Each HE provider's head of department together with a few statutory teachers (who were even less associated with specific courses, and less representative of their colleagues) were responsible for monitoring provision and scrutinising applications for course accreditation before they were sent on to National CATE. Professionalism had gone. The language of control and inspection had arrived. Most importantly, however, from the point of view of mentors, there was a new requirement of institutions to have:

> a written policy statement which sets out the roles of tutors, head-teachers, other teachers, employers and students in relation to students' school experience.
> (DES 1989, para. 2.5)

Here we see the determination to have a clearer approach to partnership than had previously been required; one that would be monitorable, measurable and able to be inspected. It is this move which has further been crystallised by the two most recent circulars about which mentors must be knowledgeable.

That year (1989) also saw the launching of the first articled teachers' pilot scheme. This was of a rather different nature from the licensed scheme, and at least still acknowledged the existence of HE. It was a two-year postgraduate form of ITT during which students spent 80% of their time in school. Courses were set up by sixteen consortia comprising local authorities and HEIs. Participants were described as teachers rather than students, and received a bursary rather than a grant. Again, it was a scheme which sought to break the mould of traditional ITE.

In 1991 two interesting reports emerged: the HMI report, *School-based initial teacher training in England and Wales* (HMI 1991) and the National Curriculum Council's (NCC) contribution to issues about partnership and the roles of the mentor and tutor, *The National Curriculum and the initial training of student, articled and licensed teachers* (NCC 1991). The HMI report examined the issue of whether ITT would be improved if it were more school-based, and looked at the practical problems associated with this. It supported the role of both college and school in ITT (referring to the HE role as 'crucial') and found (not surprisingly) that:

> the success of school-based training depends on the quality of the relationship between the training institution and the school, the significant involvement of teachers in the planning, supervision and assessment of the students' training and the active involvement of tutors in supporting the students' work in schools. In particular, it depends upon the quality of support and guidance provided for students by practising classroom teachers.
> (HMI 1991, p.3)

It also found that courses where training was predominantly in the schools were very variable, but that nevertheless given time and resources schools could play an extensive role in training. Having declared the principle of extensive school involvement 'sound', the report then recognised a number of practical problems. Here HMI showed some independence from the government line, but it was clear that this would not change the decisions already made. In any case, HMI themselves were soon to be reorganised and reduced in number.

The second document of 1991 described itself as the NCC's contribution to the current debate about the content of ITT, and as intended to be used by HE institutions, local education authorities (LEAs) and schools 'to discuss their complementary roles in preparing students to teach the national curriculum' (NCC 1991, p.3). It sets out the knowledge, understanding and skills which might reasonably be expected of all newly trained teachers in relation to the National Curriculum (NC), and suggests the opportunities and experiences which might be provided during initial training. It relates specifically to ensuring students' awareness of the NC framework; knowledge of subject content and teaching methods; skills in assessment and reporting; a view of the whole curriculum; an understanding of curriculum continuity; information technology (IT) capability; and skills in curriculum planning and review. In its essentially narrow view, this document has crystallised the totally utilitarian notion of what it is to be a teacher (NC deliverer). It is from the Appendix of this document that some of the final wording of the competences required in the following circulars was taken.

In July 1992 the Open University, encouraged by the government to the tune of 2.4 million pounds, approved a distance-learning PGCE. It originally offered 1 300 places to intending primary teachers and to subject-specific secondary teachers, and by 1994 it had 12 000 students on ITE courses. At a stroke it both extended access to the teaching profession and offered a further challenge to the traditional providers. By then all that remained was the publishing (after a brief period of consultation, during which the educational establishments' comments were ignored) of *Circular 9/92* (DFE 1992) and its Catenote (CATE 1992), which sets down in obsessive detail the criteria for secondary training, and *Circular 14/93* (DFE 1993) together with its Catenote (CATE 1993), which has done the same for the primary courses. The secondary requirements have applied to PCGE courses since September 1994, whilst the arrangements for undergraduate secondary and all primary courses apply from September 1996.

Again, for mentors, the key issues of the two similar circulars relate to the requirements for the roles of teacher and tutor. Both circulars are dedicated to ensuring that schools should play a much larger part in ITT (now as the *leading* partners in the planning and delivering of the courses) and to requiring that teachers as mentors should operate the assessment of students' teaching practice against a detailed list of competences. The details are to be found on pages 27–9, in the section dedicated specifically to these circulars.

During 1993 three HMI surveys of interest emerged: *The training of primary school teachers, March 1991 to March 1992* (OFSTED 1993a); *The licensed teacher scheme, September 1990 to July 1992* (OFSTED 1993b); and *The articled teacher scheme, September 1990 to July 1992* (OFSTED 1993c). They all bolster up the rhetoric of the earlier documents. For example, in the last of these it was made clear that the articled teacher scheme was: 'a forerunner of the move to make initial training more school-based' (OFSTED 1993c, p.23). This report claimed that an effective school-based training cannot be achieved overnight but that it is the result of sound partnerships between HEIs and schools, which take time to develop. It also calls for:

- those involved in training ... to have roles which are clearly defined and appropriate to their expertise

- trainers in schools [to] include more than mentors: all staff should be prepared for their particular contribution ...

- school and higher education institute-based training ... to be designed and implemented as one coherent course, which is organised round a well defined hierarchy of skills and understandings

- a clear and easily managed system of funding with efficient auditing procedures.
  (OFSTED 1993c, p.23)

The final moves to control all of this and to prevent access to research funding by all except those who will produce research needed by the government, are seen in the White Paper, *The government's proposals for the reform of initial teacher training* (HMSO 1993). This preceded the Education Act 1994 which in the end found the support to set up in place of CATE a Teacher Training Agency (TTA) and to begin to try to move the whole of ITT into schools by the end of the century.

This is a grim history of creeping totalitarianism and of the systematic replacement of professionalism by business mentality, orchestrated by a government determined to break what it wrongly perceives as an ideological threat and carried out by public figures who know nothing – and care nothing – about the world of schools, the future of our children, the work of teacher education and the intellectual benefits of degree-level qualifications. In short it is philistinism on a huge scale.

By the mid-1990s, then, a national ITT curriculum has been established. The scene has been set for the move from school-based ITT, where schools and HEIs work in partnership, to school-centred ITT where the school becomes the training agent, buying in other services only if it thinks fit. The absolute criteria for becoming a teacher have been pinned down in obsessive detail (obsessive because no professional work can ever be satisfactorily expressed by atomising it, but the more one attempts to do so the further one is drawn to try). And via the TTA the funding arrangements for teacher training and research have been fixed so the universities begin to withdraw from the fray, teacher preparation begins to be moved entirely into the schools, and (dangerously) all future government-funded educational research will need to be approved by the government of the day.

It is noteworthy that there has never been any debate about any of this, nor, as Edwards (1992a) points out, has there been any research into or follow-up evidence about the quality of teachers who emerge from different forms of training. Had there been debate, it is likely that the colleges would have argued for the important contribution of teachers to ITE but pointed out the range of differences between teaching and tutoring, between working with pupils and students and between what schools could offer and what the wider preparation of professionals would require. And the schools, for their part, would no doubt have argued for the recognition and use of their rich mine of expertise of practising experienced teachers, but that they should not be burdened with current responsibilities.

But none of these moves has actually been about improving the preparation of teachers. As can be seen in Stones' (1983) response to the White Paper, *Teaching quality*, the signs were clear then. The government's declared aim was to 'make the best use of *available* resources to maintain and improve standards in education'. The chief concern of the paper, though apparently about teaching quality, was in fact about the *management* of the profession, and the narrow view of teacher training already emerging from the paper was based upon 'nothing more substantial than the opinions of one or two people temporarily in high office' (Stones 1983, p.207). Stones goes on to note the 'ignorant pretentiousness' of these opinions which masquerade as concern for 'standards'.

Michael Barber echoes the point. He declares the government's policy on teacher training to be driven by two beliefs: one, the determination to limit public expenditure; the other, its ideological commitment to market forces as a means of providing the solution to public sector problems as well as those of the private sector (see Barber 1993).

Price, writing about what he calls the new *vice anglaise,* argues that the 1994 Education Act is 'directed to the cultural control of the hearts and minds of the young', and that Thatcherite policy, the educational system having been identified as a threat, sought to control 'the culture of teacher training, ... to return the teachers to the task of technical instruction; and to leave the promotion of ideology to the Government' (Price 1994, p.19).

Within ten years of the first government circular on ITT (1984), then, the take-over of ITT by schools has become the main aim of government policy. What is interesting about it is the gradual attempt to clarify what the government means by this. Wilkin offers some gloss on this (Wilkin 1990, pp.13−16). She points to the partnership of reciprocal interdependence which CNAA tried to promote and which stressed the collaboration of teachers and tutors. She discusses the partnership of equivalence as one where both parties share equally in all areas (and have no special expertise) and the partnership of complementarity as one in which each party might take responsibility for different parts of the course with a balance in overall distribution. She perceives what she calls the idea of role specialism within a framework of close collaboration in Hirst's paper, which influenced the first circular (*3/84*), but demonstrates that the partnership of equivalence rather than complementarity was actually promoted by circular. As she notes, the circular does not specify the role responsibilities, but the notion of 'recent and relevant experience' certainly suggests that teachers and tutors are the same really and that neither party has 'specific or remarkable skills'. As she observes:

> by extension, teacher training could be located in the schools with little depletion of quality since the college or department tutor has little that is unique to contribute. While the teacher must be retained, the tutor becomes marginalized if not dispensable. In this way it is suggested that Circular 3/84 presaged the direction of future government policy on teacher training.
> (Wilkin 1990, p.14)

With Catenote 4 in 1986 and *Circular 24/89*, the partnership became one-sided, and it was the teacher to whom status and authority were attributed. In fact the teacher is highlighted and the tutor hardly appears. By 1988 the lack of importance of the HEIs was then underlined by the licensed teacher scheme (where the employers of the licensee called upon HE only if they deemed it necessary). With *Circulars 9/92* and *14/93* schools are placed firmly in the lead and given the lion's share of the work. With the passing of the 1994 Education Act arrangements for schools to take over ITT altogether are enshrined in legislation. There are already some small pilot schemes in existence that are fully school-based and which use the Open University (OU) education course (Berrill 1992), and the OU's own distance-learning PGCE is also expanding. But whether many schools could find the resources and the incentives to move centre stage in ITT is however more doubtful. Harrow School publicly withdrew from school-*based* work in 1994 because of the drain on resources. It has been joined by many other schools in the London area. It seems likely, therefore, at least for the next few years that even school/college partnerships will find it a struggle to continue with the traditional ITT course structures. But, either way, the bases of these courses will be and will continue to be *Circulars 9/92* and *14/93*.

TASK 1.3: POINTS FOR REFLECTION

Alone or with a colleague

1. Write down your own experiences of supervising students and of relating in any other way to ITE. Looking at these carefully (perhaps sharing them with a colleague) what do you learn about yourself as a potential mentor?

2. What are your views about school-based and school-centred ITT? What role do you think a school should play in ITT?

3. Find out about your own school's past history of working with students and colleges over, say, the last six years. Explore these in detail. (Talk to colleagues who were involved, probe their assessment of the experiences, their values, the bases of their statements.)

(iv)

Mentoring: a close-up on government requirements

In the light of all this it is now important to explore in detail what the key circulars have to say about the partners' roles in ITT and about the possible range of relationships that can now be negotiated. The documents discussed below set out the official and extensive government requirements of mentors in both primary and secondary schools.

The secondary *Circular 9/92* (DFE 1992), which applies absolutely to all postgraduate PGCE secondary courses from September

1994 and to undergraduate secondary bachelor courses with qualified teacher status (BA/BSc/QTS secondary) from September 1996, was written with PGCE courses in mind and causes some headaches to those having to apply some of its finer details to the three- or four-year undergraduate courses.

The primary *Circular 14/93* (DFE 1993) applies absolutely to all primary courses from September 1996. Both circulars are likely to govern arrangements for mentoring in ITE for the next decade. No mentor can afford to be unfamiliar with them. In fact *Circular 14/93* is based upon *Circular 9/92* and makes few concessions to the very different nature of primary schools. For this reason a knowledge of the secondary circular and how it overlaps with the primary one is particularly useful to primary tutors and teachers.

Circular 9/92 *and Catenote*

The secondary *Circular 9/92* (paras 12, 13 and 14) declares that it expects all secondary and middle schools, sixth form and tertiary colleges in England and Wales, both maintained and independent, to have the opportunity to become partners in ITT if they wish to do so. The initiative is with the schools, who should approach HEIs. HEIs should 'make explicit ... to schools their criteria for the formation of partnerships, which should include the use of indicators as evidence of quality of teaching and learning' (DFE 1992, p.4 para. 12). Schools will be expected to describe the contributions they are able to make to the training of students and to the planning and management of courses, with particular reference to their track record in the professional development of their existing staff, school facilities, the education of children with special needs and opportunities for extracurricular activities. They should also specify the subjects they can offer and the number of students they can take. Where HEIs do not accept a school's offer of partnership, they should make clear their reasons for the decision. The Secretary of State reserves the right to withhold approval from a course if there is evidence that a school has been treated arbitrarily or unreasonably. The emphasis is said to be on 'joint responsibility for the planning and management of courses and the selection, training and assessment of students'. Yet the Circular states that the balance of responsibilities will vary. Schools will have a leading responsibility for training students to teach specialist subjects, to assess pupils and to manage classes, for supervising students and assessing their competence in these respects. To this end a set of 'competences' has been (arbitrarily) devised against which students must be assessed (see Chapters 2 and 7 below). HEIs will be responsible for ensuring that courses meet the requirements for academic validation, presenting courses for accreditation, awarding qualifications and arranging placements in more than one school. In other words the schools will do all of the work with the students, and the HEIs will do the administration.

Circular 14/93 *and Catenote*

Part 6 of this primary circular relates to the role of schools. It makes statements similar to those in *9/92* in respect of the overall responsibilities of schools for the planning and management of courses and the selection, training and assessment of students, and for the approaching of HEIs by schools who wish to become involved in ITT. It recognises that local networks of schools may be necessary because of the differences between primary and secondary schools, but it models the demands for primary partner schools on those already published for secondary (DFE 1993, p.12). But it also offers schools the chance to run their own schemes and apply direct to the DFE for funding (DFE 1993, p.8).

The Catenote declared that teachers can derive considerable professional benefit from 'sharing fully' in ITT and that they can learn from the fresh perspectives of students in training (though surely less so if they are mainly based in the school). It declares that by working in partnership with other schools and with HEIs they will gain a greater range of resources and the chance to participate more substantially in the wider community of education. It avers roundly that for individual teachers, working with students provides an important means of professional development (CATE 1993, p.4). (There is a sense here – and more so than in *9/92* – that the writers are at some pains to persuade teachers of the benefits of involvement.)

Of partnership the Catenote declares that there is no single model, but that it wishes to encourage flexibility and diversity in the development of partnership arrangements. Successful partnerships, it suggests, will:

- provide a range of expertise and resources, supplementing students' school experience as necessary from further afield

- establish and maintain coherent links between course elements in school and those in HE

- define the funding base and agree the allocation of resources

- foster professionalism for students by having school-based training as an integral part of whole school policy

- demonstrate clearly how the Circular's requirements are met. (Summary of CATE 1993, p.4)

The list of responsibilities to be shared between the partners has been taken from *Circular 9/92* and extended. Clearly these documents were written to anticipate the 1994 Education Act in their focus on profiling skills and their obsessive concern with sharpening and extending points from *Circular 9/92*. Clearly the system generally has been tightened further and further. Readers are now urged to look in detail at both circulars and their Catenotes.

Endpieces

Quality mentoring: the scope of the task

Flagged then, in both circulars and their Catenotes, are the extensively expanded roles and responsibilities of teachers. The mentoring role is quite different from previous demands on teachers. Receiving a student in school or classroom is no longer about supporting students through a single teaching practice and calling upon the tutor and the college in the event of problems. Indeed, government arrangements now require teachers to be able to debate how these professional tasks need to be divided up both in principle (in the light of ideas about what will make for quality teacher education) and pragmatically (in the light of context-specific factors relating to individual schools and their partner HEIs).

Quality teacher education and quality mentoring, then, in addition to being concerned with practical skills, means being familiar with, and knowledgeable about, both government requirements (the documents and the history) and ITE issues (including debates about the aims of teacher education and the wide range of issues that inform educational understanding). This, in turn, means that mentors will need to know their own strengths, recognise their own uncertainties and be able to debate new ways forward with an open mind from a thought-through position. Interestingly, then, by definition, a *training* for mentors would not provide the basis for fulfilling such responsibilities. That which makes for quality in both of these areas, being value-based, is complex and essentially contestable, and needs extensive and systematic exploration. By the end of this book, readers should be in a far better position to determine what makes for quality mentoring. But it is already possible to argue that what is required to prepare mentors for their work is education rather than training.

Mentor education: *developing a personal agenda*

Awareness of what one does and does not already know is a better base to proceed from than are assumptions. The following list is offered as an aid to clarifying both what is involved in mentoring and the areas in which individual mentors may need to gain new competence. Mentor education might at least include the following:

- consideration of the expertise of and possible roles for the tutor and teacher
- consideration of the rights and responsibilities of the mentor
- knowledge of government and legal matters
- awareness of partnership agreements and contractual obligations
- issues in the relationship of theory and practice
- practice in articulating and consideration of the principles of theory underlying teaching/learning
- practice in and consideration of methods of devising strategies to support the student's personal and professional development
- practice in and consideration of classroom observation for initial training and how it relates both to observation and mentoring for newly qualified teachers (NQTs) and to staff appraisal
- practice in and consideration of a range of approaches for responding to a lesson (reflection/enabling student to theorise/feedback/critique)
- practice in and consideration of assessing student competence in the classroom
- practice in and consideration of operating competence profiling procedures and drawing up recommendations for future training

- practice in and consideration of developing relevant inter-personal skills

- detailed knowledge about how student courses are planned and awareness of the kinds of questions to ask about course design and about the specific course for which mentoring is being offered

- issues about what constitutes professional knowledge and educational understanding beyond classroom skills

- issues relating to the student and the whole school

- issues relating to students and professionalism

- preparation for the selection of candidates for training

- issues in quality control, including course evaluation.

You may wish to add other items.

To some extent much of the rest of this book is an attempt to begin to come to grips with these matters. Since what is offered here is quality mentoring, based upon mentor education, the following two chapters focus upon further important issues as a basis for the more practical elements which appear in Part 2 of the book. Before turning to these, however, it is important to construct an agenda of your own in order to come to grips personally with what is offered and to know what you seek particularly from the following pages. The tasks below should help you to do this. The 'Further reading' relates to the main substance of the chapter. There is no substitute for having read and annotated your own copies of the circulars that are relevant to you.

TASK 1.4: POINTS FOR ACTION

Alone or with a colleague
1. List any matters that you would like to learn more about in relation to the HEI's roles in ITE. Consider how you might gain this information.
2. In the light of this chapter (particularly the list above) and your own reflections, list your personal targets for learning to be a mentor.*

* This list may be of interest to you again later. You may wish to review and/or refine it as you proceed through the book. You may wish to return to it at the end.

Further reading

A: Government circulars

CATE (November 1992) *The accreditation of initial teacher training under Circulars 9/92 (Department For Education) and 34/92 (Welsh Office): a note of guidance.* London: CATE.
CATE (November 1993) *The initial training of primary school teachers (Circular 14/93) (England): a note of guidance.* London: CATE.
DFE (1992) *Initial teacher training (secondary phase) (Circular 9/92).* London: DFE.
DFE (1993) *The initial training of primary school teachers: new criteria for courses (Circular 14/93).* London: DFE.

It is also important to read any documents which are already in your school relating to student teachers and which have come from your specific HE provider.

B: Other useful articles/chapters

Edwards, T. (1992a) *Change and reform in initial teacher education (Briefing Paper 9).* London: National Commission on Education.
Fish, D. (1989) *Learning through practice in initial teacher training.* London: Kogan Page (see particularly pp.21–47).
Gardner, P. (1993) 'The early history of school-based teacher training', in McIntyre, D., Haggar, H. and Wilkin, M. (Eds) (1993) *Mentoring: perspectives on school-based teacher education.* London: Kogan Page, pp.21–36.
Wilkin, M. (1990) 'The development of partnership in the United Kingdom', in Booth, M., Furlong, J. and Wilkin, M. (Eds) (1990) *Partnership in initial teacher training.* London: Cassell, pp.3–23.

CHAPTER 2

Quality in Professional Practice: Considering Professionalism

Introduction

The word 'professional' is much bandied about in debates about ITE. Students are involved in ITE in order to join a profession. In schools it is often the (vague) notional standard against which students are held: 'We expect professionals to ...' What is being judged at the end of a course is the quality of professional practice. In their own work mentors are expected to offer evidence of quality professional practice in teaching pupils *and* in working with student teachers. They have become the gatekeepers to a profession.

But beneath the slippery words 'profession' and 'professional' lies a number of complexities about which mentors need to be clear. Indeed, without a clear grasp of differing models of professionalism, and a thought-through position on their own preferred approach, mentors' work with students is likely to lack sharp direction, and they will be unable to discuss it fully with those responsible for monitoring the quality of ITE.

Teachers who act as mentors, then, need to be familiar with the issues and debates associated with professionalism and being a member of a profession for at least four major reasons.

1. In helping student teachers to become members of a profession, mentors are engaged in professional education, and need to be clear what this enterprise involves.

2. Discussions between a mentor and a student are almost always bound to touch on issues about becoming a professional,

professionalism, and the teaching profession. Even if these are not the main topic they may underlie it.

3. Since professions generally are much under attack in the media, students, as a direct part of their education, need to address the notion of professionalism and need to be prepared to discuss it with colleagues, parents and governors.

4. Most importantly, views about professionalism (what it is to be a professional, what professionals should know and do, and how professionals think and behave) determine the kind of education mentors offer to students, and it is crucial that mentors are aware of this, make a rational choice about it and are able to defend that choice.

What is a profession? What is professionalism?

A profession is a body of practitioners who offer public service for the public good, rather than working with products for their own profit. This indicates clearly that there is a strong moral dimension to professionalism. To be a professional is to have expert know-how underpinned by theoretical knowledge at graduate or graduate-equivalent level. The 'good' emanating from this knowledge and accruing to individual clients must be distributed fairly and disinterestedly. Becoming a member of a profession is achieved by being approved and accepted (given professional status) as a result of examination in both practical and theoretical dimensions of knowledge by those who are already members of the body. That approval traditionally rests not on a demonstration of mastery as a result of training but on evidence of the ability to exercise professional judgement as a result of education. Such a professional must maintain personal standards of theoretical and practical knowledge, discipline and ethical behaviour (although there is also usually an overseeing professional council which ensures standards). Professional practitioners must operate effectively and conduct themselves appropriately according to the purposes and procedures that are traditional to the profession. Central to these traditions is the (currently unfashionable) concept of service. Professionals are thus autonomous operators in that within professional parameters they must, during practice, make considerable use of their personal judgement in making decisions. There is a moral dimension to this decision-making precisely because the professional's goal is to offer public service for public good.

Schön, writing from an American context, argues that the status of all professions is being eroded (Schön 1983 and 1987). He puts this down to the fact that professions had a contract with society that in return for reliable public service they were granted autonomy, self-regulation and a certain amount of secrecy. But they have lost their status and contract because in this age of consumerism and its resulting accountability, and at a time when authority is questioned everywhere, some professionals have been shown to have made major mistakes and to have let their clients down. He evidences the many legal cases in America. These have caused society to call for the withdrawal of professional privileges and perhaps to accord a different and much looser meaning to the word professional. Certainly Goodyear makes the point that:

> the meaning of 'professional' has slid away from the rich suggestiveness of, say, 'professional judgement', or 'professional integrity' towards the narrower end of its continuum, where it is synonymous with 'proficient', as in 'they made a very professional job of it'. (Goodyear 1992, p.396)

Nevertheless, there are still areas of employment that are generally recognised as professional. Significant examples are law and medicine. It is, however, a matter of dispute as to whether teaching is a profession of the same kind as these (see Langford 1978). Given the constant intervention by government over the content and procedures of teaching, it is certainly not an autonomous and self-regulating profession in the way that these are. Given the government's view of teaching as operating routines, the fact that many see teachers as deliverers of a curriculum decided by those outside the profession, the changing of teachers' pay and conditions, the fact that teachers are not permitted a professional body to regulate their affairs, and the fact that preparation for the profession is now referred to as training, it is certainly doubtful whether teaching is *regarded* as a profession.

Yet, at the level of the important moral dimension, there is much that can be said very clearly about teachers being educational professionals. For example, teachers are clearly responsible for the distribution of important benefits, they seek to improve others, they are involved in endless autonomous rational judgements, they must demonstrate professional disinterest, and they must work with, rather than on, their clients in order to enable them to recognise and to come to understand their very educational needs. In David Carr's terms they are involved in the provision of 'ethically grounded, essentially consultative, public service' (Carr, D. 1992, p.22). He makes the further point that whilst teachers need important classroom skills, these:

> cannot be happily disengaged from wider considerations of a philo-
> sophical, moral or evaluative kind about the precise nature of the
> benefit which we are trying to provide for children through education
> and about our larger purposes as educationalists with respect to that
> benefit.
> (Carr, D. 1992, p.20)

He also reminds us that craft skills take on their proper significance only:

> as enmeshed in a wider context of aims and objectives which are
> defined by reference to a complex network of public, social and
> moral duties and obligations which the teacher owes to children,
> parents, employing authorities and society at large.
> (Carr, D. 1992, p.22)

Significantly he also emphasises that to be prepared for this role
student teachers will require:

> the kind of *education* which will equip them with capacities for
> autonomous judgement and action – to render them capable of
> reliable, responsible and informed decisions about what lies in the
> best interests of those whom they are in the business to serve.
> (Carr, D. 1992, p.22)

In respect of differing kinds of educational professionals, it is possible, following Hoyle, to distinguish between extended and restricted professionals. He suggests in a seminal article about teachers, that, unlike restricted professional teachers who place value on pure experience in isolation from broad understanding of education and from colleagues, extended professionals are those who seek to understand their practice by considering theory and seeking broader contexts. They see classroom events in relation to social policies and goals. They share methods and ideas with colleagues, and value collaboration. They value the opportunity to be creative rather than use teacher-proofed packages. They read professional literature, are involved in in-service education (INSET) and staff development, and see teaching as an intuitive, rather than a rational, activity (see Hoyle 1974).

Various authors since Hoyle have offered further sophistication of the characteristics of the extended professional, particularly in respect of being a professional who investigates his/her personal professional practice (see Stenhouse 1975), and those of being a reflective teacher (an idea based on the original work of Schön 1983).

What is professional knowledge?

Pressures, arising from accountability, to 'state everything' about public services have led to attempts to list comprehensively all aspects of professional knowledge and to use that list to judge those entering the profession. But such lists are misleading. The whole point about professionalism is that it is not possible to set down simply a generally agreed, detailed statement about a professional's knowledge-base. The essentially human and unique character of interaction between a professional and clients make the detailed knowledge needed in each interaction unpredictable. A professional needs to be able to operate professional judgement and select or even create knowledge necessary to the unique situation. The only way to prepare for this is by offering the student a broad education. It is also important to note that professional knowledge is far from static, but that it changes rapidly as new discoveries are made. These discoveries are often the fruits of research. Such research is seen as an important *part of* practitioners' practice, not as something offered to practitioners by outside researchers. And so research activity and its resulting knowledge are important cutting edges for developing professional practice. The whole issue of professionalism and preparation for becoming a professional is thus highly complex and to try to simplify it is to distort it.

TASK 2.1: POINTS FOR REFLECTION

Alone or with a colleague
1.   Is teaching a profession? What are your views so far about professionalism?

2.   On what sort of occasions, in what contexts and why, do you yourself use the word professional? What do you normally mean by it?

3.   What do you think of Hoyle's models of extended and restricted professionals?

4.   How would you describe the key characteristics of your own professionalism?

So here we have begun to ascertain why educating student teachers is a difficult matter. There are conflicting views about what kind of professional a teacher now is, what they should know and be able to do, and how they should be prepared for future employment. The following is an attempt to demonstrate these issues in more detail. The discussion provides a rationale for the rest of this book and a challenge to all who work with student teachers to consider their own stance towards being a professional and preparing others to enter the profession.

Two models of professional practice explored

Some people, then, see the preparation for teaching as offering would-be professionals a set of clear-cut routines and behaviours and pre-packaged course content which requires only an efficient means of delivery. This cuts down considerably, they argue, the risks that professionals might fail to provide a reliable service. This attitude in turn makes assumptions that teaching and learning are relatively simple interactions in which the teacher gives out and pupils take in. Others, however, feel that such a position denies the real character of both professionalism on the one hand and teaching and learning on the other. They argue that teaching involves complex decision-making and elements of professional judgement and practical wisdom, all guided by moral principles, but that these are not able to be set down in absolute routines.

One view of professionalism characterises professional activities as essentially simple, describable and able to be broken down into their component parts (skills) and thus mastered. It regards being a professional as being essentially efficient in skills, and submissive in harnessing them to carry out other people's decisions. (In this case the decision is that education should be a market-led service which prepares pupils to play their parts in a wealth-creating society.) This means 'the job of the teacher being redefined along the lines of a technician' (Kydd and Weir 1993, p.409). This in turn means teachers being answerable only for the technical accuracy of their work within the bounds of achieving other people's goals. In other words, the professional's role is purely instrumental. This is the TR view of professional practice. It has at its base what Raymond Williams described as the industrial trainers' approach to education (Williams 1965).

It can be seen as diametrically opposed to the view in which behaving professionally is seen as being concerned with both means and ends. Here, the end is that of liberal education. Here professional activity is more akin to artistry; practitioners are broadly autonomous, making their own decisions about their actions and the moral bases of those actions. In this model the professional is not less accountable, but is in fact more so. Here, to be professional is to be morally accountable for all of one's conduct. Here the ability to exercise professional judgement is seen as essential. And professional judgement is not a simple skill. In fact this view of professional practice rejects the notion that it can be divided into simple skills. It considers that professional activity includes components which cannot be entirely disentangled and treated separately. It takes a more holistic view. This has been called the professional artistry view (see Schön 1987).

In all of this, then, questions are raised about what professional expertise should consist of and therefore what professionals should do in order to learn and then to improve their practice.

Some would argue that professional practice has for too long been surrounded by a mystique and that we have now advanced to the point where goals can be set by society for professionals whose role is purely instrumental. This role can now be analysed (technically and rationally) in terms of the activities and skills (the professional craft knowledge) and all that remains is to teach these to the professional trainee. Here, to learn professional practice is to identify and then to practise skills until they have been mastered, and then to learn to apply them with success to real situations. The language is not about professional *competence* (a holistic concept) but of individual *competences* (an atomising of skills). To improve practice is to move on to harder skills and more complex situations. This offers an incremental view of practice. The fact that many of these competences are simple and can be quickly taught, simply practised and easily measured or observed is also regarded as entirely desirable in a world of reducing resources.

By contrast, however, some would argue that the TR view of professionalism, which offers simple pre-set routines and procedures, skills and knowledge, does not meet the real situations of practice. They would emphasise the idea that practice is messy, unpredictable, unexpected, and requires the ability to improvise (an ability often *diminished* by training and routine). In short it requires professional artistry well beyond technical efficiency or routine craft skills. Also, practice is rapidly changing and requires the practitioner autonomously to be able to refine and update his/her expertise 'on the hoof'. The problem seen with the TR approach to professional practice is that it simply leads in the end to an obsessive intention to tie things down further and further in the inevitably vain attempt to try to cater for all eventualities. By contrast, professional artistry sees the practitioner as being educated roundly, not drilled in skills. To improve practice is to treat it more holistically, to work to understand its complexities and to look carefully at one's actions and theories as one works. Subsequently, it is necessary to challenge them with ideas from other perspectives, and to seek to improve and refine practice and its underlying theory. Here the professional is working towards increased competence. Some would argue that this is all too woolly (because it admits of less certainty). Further, it does not please politicians because its fruits may show up less clearly in the short term since it emphasises aspects that are not simple visible behaviours. But it offers in the long term scope for more deeply rooted improvements, which are owned by the professional.

Thus, the TR view enshrines the centrality of rules, schedules, prescriptions, whereas those holding the professional artistry (PA) view believe that practice starts where the rules fade (because the rules rarely fit real practice). Instead of prescriptions, the PA view relies on frameworks and rules of thumb. The TR view emphasises diagnosis, analysis and efficient systems. It values detailed job specifications and being able to analyse a professional role down to the last detail. The PA view, by contrast, believes instead in interpretation of details, acknowledges the inevitable subjectivity of setting them down, and comes to an understanding of professional activities by means of appreciation (as in the critical appreciation of art and music). It wishes to encourage not narrow efficiency but creativity and the right to be wrong. The TR model assumes that knowledge is permanent, able to be encompassed totally and thus worth attempting to master. The PA view is that knowledge is temporary, dynamic and problematic and that knowing processes is more useful than knowing facts.

Their impact on practice and theory

But it is, perhaps, in views about theory that the TR model is most highly specific. It sees theory as 'formal theory' produced by researchers (who stand apart from the practitioners). This formal theory is to be learnt and then applied to practice. It regards practice as an arena in which to demonstrate previously worked-out theory. This view, that theory is formal and applicatory, is what has led in the past to the old traditional approach to professional education in which the first three-quarters of the training course is carried out in college and the 'application' of all the knowledge so gained is put into practical operation in the school only at the end of the course. By contrast, the PA view is that theory is implicit in (underlies) all action, that both action and theory are developed in practice, that refining practice involves unearthing the theories on which it is founded and that formal theory aids the development of practice by challenging and extending the practitioner's understanding. This view, that (with the help of reflection) theory emerges *from* practice, enables the professional training course to begin with *practice*, and to enable the student to examine and develop personal theory as it arises from that practice. Such personal theory is implicit in all action but needs to be exhumed from it in order that it can be acknowledged, understood and used to inform decisions about later action. It is also able to be refined by recourse to further practice and to the wider view of theory offered by other theorists and researchers. Chapters 3, 4 and 6 illustrate this in much more detail and provide practical assistance for mentors in how to consider their own practice and to how to enable students to do the same.

Their views of professional activities

There are other characteristics that distinguish the two different views of professionalism enshrined in these models. These consist of views about and attitudes to professional activity. For example, the TR view believes in the mastery of skills and knowledge, and regards the process of becoming a professional as the acquisition of sets of competences which can be taught by training. The TR view, then, emphasises the 'known' and is in tune with present trends in that it celebrates certainty and hard evidence as opposed to uncertainty, humility and critical scepticism. Professional practice in this model is made up from a series of definable skills, measurable by means of observation, and influenced by researchers from outside the teaching profession.

By contrast the PA view is willing to accept the notion of mystery within human activity. It regards the activity of the professional as not entirely able to be analysed down to the last atom even if the routine craft skills on which artistry is based are able to be specified (see Brown and McIntyre 1993). It regards professional practitioners as eternal seekers rather than 'knowers'. It sees the activities of the professional as mainly open capacities which by definition cannot be mastered. The test of an open capacity is that the learner can take steps which she/he has not been taught to take, which in some measure surprise the teacher, that she/he can 'do the unexpected, ... do it well, efficiently and at the right time' (Passmore 1980, pp.42–3). The PA view then, sees professional practice as an art in which risks are inevitable, learning to do is achieved only by engaging in doing (together with reflection upon the doing), and where improvisation, enquiry into action and resulting insight by those involved in it generate a major knowledge base.

Their differing views of quality

Each model gives rise to a particular view of quality. The TR model speaks in the language of quality control. It places emphasis upon visible performance within the practical aspects of the course. It seeks to test and measure these, believing that technical expertise is all-important and that learning cashes out immediately into visible products. Thus the model is behaviourist, emphasises fixed standards, controls the course via inspection and appraisal, and believes that change can be imposed from outside the profession and that quality is measurable. It wishes to hold the professional practitioner accountable only for his/her technical expertise.

By contrast, the PA view sees that there is more to professional practice than its surface and visible features. It takes the view that there is more to the whole than the sum of the parts, it believes in professional judgements, and holds that the most easily measurable is often the most trivial. Further, it wishes to harness investigation, reflection and deliberation in order to enable professionals to develop their own insights from inside, and it sees this as a better means of staff development than innovation imposed from without. In short, it believes that quality comes from deepening insight into one's own values, priorities, actions. Under this model it is possible to talk about wide professional answerability rather than narrow technical accountability. This introduces not only a responsibility for the moral dimensions of professional action, but also the responsibility to reflect upon, investigate and refine one's own practice. (The following table offers a summary of the points above.)

To look closely at these two very different views of professionalism is to recognise between them some clear incompatibilities. Some argue that these views are extreme versions of a continuum along which individuals can find their own place. Some hold them to

Table 2.1 Two models of professionalism

The TR view	*The PA view*
Follows rules, laws, schedules; uses routines, prescriptions	Starts where rules fade; see patterns, frameworks
Uses diagnosis/analysis to think about teaching	Uses interpretation and appreciation to think about teaching
Wants efficient systems	Wants creativity and room to be wrong
Sees knowledge as graspable, permanent	Sees knowledge as temporary, dynamic, problematic
Theory is applied to practice	Theory emerges from practice
Visible performance is central	There is more to it than surface features
Setting out and testing for basic competences is vital	There is more to teaching than the sum of the parts
Technical expertise is all	Professional judgement counts
Sees professional activities as masterable	Sees mystery at the heart of professional activities
Emphasises the known	Embraces uncertainty
Standards must be fixed; standards are measurable; standards must be controlled	That which is most easily fixed and measurable is also trivial – professionals should be trusted
Emphasises assessment, appraisal, inspection, accreditation	Emphasises investigation, reflection, deliberation
Change must be managed from outside	Professionals can develop from inside
Quality is really about quantity of that which is easily measurable	Quality comes from deepening insight into one's values, priorities, actions
Technical accountability	Professional answerability
This is training	This is education
Takes the instrumental view of learning	Sees education as intrinsically worthwhile

be ultimately antithetical, requiring harder decisions to be made about where one stands. It is important to consider these positions carefully because the models themselves give rise to two distinct approaches to teacher education which are found extensively in current ITE courses – and in the literature about them. And it is these approaches which in turn colour and shape practice in ITE on the ground. To work as a mentor with student teachers is to take a stand on these matters – whether consciously or not! Students too are aware of these models, and preparation to teach includes consideration of them. Mentors may find it impossible to offer a rationale for their practice and to cope with student queries about practice without recourse to these issues and a clear idea of their own views about them. Quality mentoring certainly demands no less.

TASK 2.2: POINT FOR REFLECTION

Models are dangerous in their simplification and polarising of issues. This is because they are reductionist. That is, they reduce matters to crude elements that do not do justice to the complexities found in practice. They are useful only if, by highlighting and emphasising differences, they enable issues to be considered which will then enlighten practice.

● What are your views so far about the models presented in this chapter?

Two models of teacher education

The TR model of professionalism has given rise to the competency-based approach to ITE. The PA view of professionalism underlies the reflective practitioner philosophy of teacher education. Many, indeed most, current ITE courses were designed on the basis of the reflective practitioner philosophy. (See the Modes of Teacher Education Research Project Survey of ITE carried out in 1992 (Barrett *et al.* 1992).)

The government has espoused the TR model, though apparently not from any view that it makes for better preparation of teachers but simply because it is cheaper and, being performance-based, yields more easily to industrial notions of quality control. It has now required (without any debate) all courses to take as their goals (aims) a set of prescribed competences (one list for all secondary students, and a slightly different list for all primary students).

This is an attempt to standardise courses. Most courses, unwilling to give up entirely their thought-through philosophy of how to prepare intending teachers, have retained as much as possible of their reflective practitioner approach and grafted on to this the required competences. (It is interesting to note that the competences required by the government have been backed by absolute threat to withdraw accreditation from, and therefore to close, any course that fails to implement them. Such a move speaks for itself in revealing government attitudes to professionals and in the recourse to force rather than rational argument.) As a result of these moves there are fragments of both philosophies in most ITE courses. This does cause a number of tensions, however, since for some people at least, the two approaches are incompatible. At best they do not sit easily together by virtue of their opposing views about the basic nature of the task of preparing professional practitioners. The details of the differing approaches are now offered below. Mentors will wish to consider them carefully.

Competency-based teacher education

At root, competency-based teacher education treats teaching as if it were an occupation rather than a profession. Education is seen in terms of an industrial transaction where what is important is the efficient and cheap delivery of a product (the National Curriculum). Here practice is not simply of prime importance; it is the *only* important focus. Theory (of any kind) is not regarded as important. What matters most in training for this job is mastering specific and standardised skills and demonstrating that mastery. The skills are thus turned into competences and used as the means of assessing performance in the workplace. Such an approach, though useful in factory production where there is only one right way of doing things and professional judgement is irrelevant, is incompatible with professional activity. In teaching it is different. Dividing teaching into collections of skills which can be seen and measured distorts the nature of teaching because there is much more to being a professional teacher than that, nor will there be universal agreement about exactly how many skills are necessary. For example:

- How and from where will such skills be derived? (On the basis of which model of teaching will they be chosen?)

- How explicitly and in what detail should they be defined?

- How many should there be?

- What will count as evidence for their acquisition? (How many times must they be demonstrated before they are deemed to have been acquired?)

- Will students need to pass them all, and should they strive to pass each at the same level?

- What order of priority (weighting) will they be given, and how?

- How will experience affect the level expected? (Should NQTs have to demonstrate less than the full range, and if so which should be left till later?)

The arguments for competency-based approaches to ITT spring from a bureaucratic desire to pin down what teachers should learn in order to be able to observe and measure them and thus account for them. For some, however, the price of doing so is too high, and the gains from the attempt are less useful than bureaucrats would have us believe.

The Training Agency, employing management jargon from industry and defining occupation competency, offers us a chilling version of what measuring competences is about and shows how the notion of simple observable measures of job efficiency is difficult even in a more streamlined work environment. It argues that 'occupational competence':

> stems from an understanding [that] to perform effectively in a work role, an individual has to combine:
>
> - performance of various technical and task components
>
> - overarching management of the various technical and task components to achieve the overall work function
>
> - management of the variance and unpredictability in the work role and wider environment
>
> - integration of the work role within the context of the wider organisational, economic, market and social environment.
>
> (Training Agency 1988: quoted in Burke 1989, p.190)

A CNAA document on teacher education however concedes that:

> A narrow definition based on observable workplace skills is certainly in some tension with the rationale of a liberal education and even

> with the notion of the reflective professional. On the other hand, a
> broader definition can make it difficult to define criteria of compe-
> tence in any meaningful way.
> (CNAA 1992a, p.7)

This, disturbingly, shows a willingness to accept the notion that
the liberal educational and the narrower training approach to
ITE are essentially of equal worth. This damaging view would
have been roundly rejected in the mid-1980s as ignoring the vital
moral dimension to teaching. How has it been allowed to become
so acceptable now?

It probably springs from a failure to distinguish between 'competence' (a broad ability, which no one would wish to disown as part
of professionalism) and the quite different notion of 'competences'
or 'competency' (individual skills which atomise teaching). The work
of David Carr shows that the first of these, 'competence', is the
wider and more holistic, and is understood in the *capacity* sense:
'capacities entail the voluntary and deliberate exercise of principled
judgement in the light of rational knowledge and understanding'
(see Carr, D. 1993, p.257). It is the result, then, of education. The
second is narrower, more atomistic and could be understood in the
dispositional sense. (Dispositions include skills, faculties, habits
and are caused by innate ability or training.) He indicates that it is
easy to relate and confuse the two (particularly when the singular
('competence') is used as a dispositional term), but that for the
preparation of teachers it is vital to hold them apart. And clearly
there is a world of difference between thinking about teaching in
terms of pre-specifiable discrete itemised skills (competences) on the
one hand and behaviour resulting from an educated understanding
(competence) on the other. It is a distinction, as Carr says, between:

> doing in a broadly principled, reflective and informed way and doing
> well, efficiently or effectively according to some verifiable canon or
> standard of acceptable performance.
> (Carr, D. 1993, p.262)

Clearly, as he shows, the two aspects of competence *ought* to go
together, and some see the broader view as subsumed in the narrower
one. But it is more complex than this. A reflective practitioner might
perform badly in terms of dispositional effectiveness but be able to
reflect upon and refine practice, whereas an effective practitioner
who performs routinely well but has no principled understanding
might never develop further. The former might he helped by practising
skills. The latter is avoided only by a reflective approach to practice
(see also Fish 1995). Carr concludes that:

> professional competence in the capacity sense cannot be reduced to a set of competences in the dispositional sense ... It is a crucial component of professional competence to profess and exhibit certain moral values such as a respect for persons; but if I fail to show respect for a child it is not a failure of a *technical skill* that is here in question.
> (Carr, D. 1993, p.264)

There are problems then, and pros and cons to be weighed, in adopting this approach. In summary, I would wish to argue, then, that the invention of competences as the means of assessment in teacher education are an attempt to:

- substitute the notion of competences for the notion of competence and thus reduce the status and significance of professionalism

- simplify the problematic (as if teaching is merely a matter of learning a few skills and strategies)

- make 'plain sense' out of the genuinely complex (as if the skills and strategies sought are straightforward and are known and agreed by everyone)

- present knowledge as absolute when much is still unknown (as if everyone knows how children learn when much is value-based *theory*)

- de-politicise the essentially political (as if matters beyond acquiring and using the basic skills and knowledge set out are not the business of teachers)

- render amoral the deeply moral (as if there are no issues at stake beneath these skills about what is − and what is not − offered to pupils to learn in school)

- universalise the eternally contestable (as if teaching skills and strategies are not only agreed by everyone but are applicable in every situation)

- pretend the possibility of objectivity in the face of certain subjectivity (as if, because the competences are now set out clearly and must be used on every course, every student will now be assessed in the same way and against the same standard, and that thus, subjectivity has either already been eradicated or soon will be by means of quality control).

The invention of competences appears to offer simple measures of efficiency. Yet such apparently sure foundations are easily revealed as false. How ironic it will be, then, if institutions are driven by government coercion in the name of 'improving' quality control to ditch the moral dimensions in ITE, as found in the reflective practitioner approach, in favour of (cheaper) simple approaches concerned only with technical accountability. However, since they are a government requirement, it is important that mentors understand how to assess by means of them. Chapter 7 below focusses upon this in great detail, providing a range of practical possibilities.

TASK 2.3: POINTS FOR ACTION AND REFLECTION

1. Look at the competences for student teachers in *Circular 9/92* or *14/93*.
   a. Comment on how you would fare if you were assessed against them (for one lesson/across a week of lessons).
   b. What else is important to consider in assessing a teacher's competence?
2. Under what circumstances might competences stress performance at the expense of understanding?
3. Is it reasonable to label as competences knowledge, values, attitudes, personal attributes?
4. Where, in competency-based training, does the learner's motivation come from?
5. List the competences that mentors might be asked to master. Now compare your list with the list on pages 30–1 above and with your own personal agenda produced at the end of Chapter 1. Make a note about what you discover.

Although competences are a requirement of all ITE programmes, many courses retain at least some of the elements of the other main approach to which we shall now turn.

Reflective practitioner philosophy

The arguments for taking a reflective practitioner approach to ITE are derived from the PA view of teaching. Broadly the arguments are as follows.

The world of professional practice is fast changing. Professionals need to exercise and to continue to refine and develop not only simple skills, but their own dispositions, personality/professional character, abilities, capacities, understandings. Many aspects of teaching a lesson cannot be pre-specified. Professionals need to be able to think on their feet, to improvise, to respond to the uncharted and unpredictable. Further, teaching is a moral and social practice requiring the ability to exercise moral decision-making and professional judgement. What is needed is an approach to teaching and to learning to teach which enables teachers 'to work at their practice, modify it and keep it under critical control' (Eraut 1989, p.175). Critical consciousness which unearths personal theories enables practice (both in new situations and familiar ones) to be modified and improved. He argues that once one becomes more aware of the nature and effect of one's own theories, then it is possible to consider those of others. Equally, by recognising the contexts in which one has developed one's theories one is better able to judge when new theories are needed to cope with new kinds of contexts (see Eraut 1989, p.184).

When a course claims that the underlying course philosophy is that of the reflective practitioner it means far more than the rather obvious point that we should all think about what we do as practising professionals. Some argue that Schön's version of reflection (Schön 1983 and 1987) is inherently conservative in that it does not involve radical challenge to the practitioner's values and views, but merely expects the practitioner to oscillate between action and thought. But this need not be so. Indeed, the term reflective practice has been coined to imply quite the opposite – that the practitioner will investigate practice and draw up to it a range of perspectives from theory. There is also dispute about the exact meaning of this term reflective practitioner (see Calderhead 1988 and 1989; Russell 1993b). Calderhead points to the fact that many terms exist – like 'reflective practice', 'enquiry-oriented teacher education', 'teacher as researcher', 'teacher as decision-maker', 'teacher as problem-solver' – and that all of these embrace the notion of reflection, but add to it a range of other and differing ideas. He also draws attention to the fact that the key theorists on whose work the notion of reflective practice is based include Dewey and Schön. He shows that reflective teaching has 'become a slogan, disguising numerous practices' (Calderhead 1989, p.46) and that there is as yet no clear language in which to discuss these matters. Reflective practice, then, is a developing concept, in need of further refinement, and subject at the moment to particular pressures from an antithetical climate.

Nevertheless, it seems to have offered a common enough set of characteristics for those in ITE to see its character as including:

- taking practice *and* personal and formal theory seriously and being aware of their complexities

- taking a holistic view of professional practice

- taking a problem-solving stance to practice

- recognising the need for the practitioner to investigate practice personally and valuing small-scale humanistic enquiry

- seeking the 'meaning in the experience' by means of reflecting on it

- seeking to identify beneath practice the values, assumptions, beliefs and personal theories (or 'theories of action')

- working in collaboration with colleagues, the better to reflect, deliberate and understand practice

- doing all of this in order to develop/change/refine/challenge practice.

Since the term 'reflection' is central to this approach, it is also important to understand something of its nature within this context and to try to be clear about how it relates to other similar concepts.

Reflection is one means of investigating practice and of theorising about it. Basically it involves systematic critical and creative thinking about action with the intention of understanding its roots and processes and thus being in a position to refine, improve or change future actions. It is related to, but different from evaluation, deliberation, appraisal and self-appraisal.

Appraisal and self-appraisal might be described as interested in the (immediate) success of the professional practitioners' *performance*. Evaluation and self-evaluation might be seen as seeking evidence which will enable practitioners to measure the results of a course against its objectives. Deliberation is described by Schwab as a process of corporate discussion about future actions based upon weighing data and professional judgements. Reflection, on the other hand, whilst sharing with the others a research/investigative base, and being, like them, a response to quality control issues and an aid in the attempt to improve future actions, is unlike them in that it demonstrates an interest in:

- understanding the interrelated processes of the particular thought and action, rather than displaying the surface features

- identifying the personal theories of the practitioner and considering how they might be refined

- recognising the values and beliefs that underlie the particular practitioner's actions.

In these respects reflection touches matters that are both more intimate and more difficult to acknowledge than are other approaches to investigating practice, like some forms of action research. Arguably also, it unearths issues that are at the very centre of understanding and refining our own practice.

There is not one but a number of ways in which we can reflect upon action. Schön has pointed out that reflection can take place during the action itself (this he calls reflection-in-action) and/or it can take place after the action as a result of looking back upon it (this he calls reflection-on-action) (see Schön 1987). Chapter 6 below looks at these concepts in detail.

This view of professional practice raises deep questions about what kind of professional expertise (professional body of knowledge) professionals need to learn, what their educators need to foster in them and what their assessors need to monitor. Given the notion that teaching is a kind of practical problem-solving where teachers seek to understand inevitably unique situations to which they have to offer a creative response, how can students be educated to do this and how can that education be assessed? (Clearly they cannot be *trained* for the unexpected.) What we are talking about is creating conditions for, and a means of monitoring, the development of professional artistry. What *is* the relevant expertise then that students are trying to acquire, and how can we provide for it?

The expertise sought is practical wisdom and professional judgement. It might best be achieved by wide-ranging education in addition to practice in specific skills. Such education would aim at providing something of the following:

- appreciation of the complexities of practice and how that practice is learnt

- the ability and capacity to investigate practice

- the ability and capacity to refine practice

- the ability and capacity to theorise from practice

- the ability and capacity to reflect on practice in a systematic and rigorous way

- an understanding of the complexity of the relationship between thought and action

- knowledge of formal theory and of how to harness it to enlighten practice.

In short, they need to learn the art of the practical (ways of harnessing theory and practice) by means of practice and practical discourse. And ways have to be found of assessing this and of dividing the successful from the unsuccessful practitioners.

The remaining chapters of this book attempt to look in detail at how mentors can provide these conditions, and carry out such assessment.

Implications for mentor and tutor

The implications for the teacher/mentor and tutor of the competency-based approach to ITT are that both parties' main tasks are to prepare students in practice to demonstrate the behaviour/skills delineated in the government circulars. They must take a behaviourist approach to both the student's practice and their own with pupils and with students. They must be able to demonstrate that they themselves possess these skills (hence the requirement of tutors that they have 'recent and relevant' teaching experience). A major focus for their discussions with students will be the visible behaviour they have observed. There are also no real distinctions needed in this approach to ITT between what teacher and tutor actually offer students. It assumes reciprocal partnership. Indeed, in time the tutor's only role will be to support the teacher.

It would be possible to train students on this basis with relatively little recourse to the theoretical aspects of teaching. There need be no reference to the students' theories, assumptions or beliefs that underlie and inform their practice. There need be no discussion of the decision-making that has informed practice, beyond the simple technical decisions about the means adopted in a particular lesson. The culmination of such training would be that the student would be helped by teacher and tutor ultimately to take over the process of self-evaluation against the list of competences given and become a self-directing technical practitioner. Relatively little is required of teacher and tutor beyond this. And so relatively little is gained (for either teacher or school) by being involved in ITT. They will be the proverbial Nelly with whom the student will sit!

The demands on teachers and tutors of adopting the reflective practice philosophy, on the other hand, are considerable. Those offering professional education shaped by this philosophy will need to have certain skills and will adopt certain responsibilities. As a result they will also gain enormously in terms of their own professional development and the whole school will become a self-reflecting, self-developing institution. The reflective practice approach assumes that supervisors and mentors have the knowledge and skills to operate as reflective practitioners themselves – that they can unearth the theory beneath their practice, challenge it with ideas drawn from other perspectives, refine it and investigate the refinements. It assumes that those supervising students' practice will be able to work with students to help them tackle the complex matters of their educational aims and will be able to encourage them to face up to their uncertainties as well as their need to reconsider their values.

The following chapters are an attempt to explore some of these issues in greater detail.

TASK 2.4: POINTS FOR ACTION AND REFLECTION

1. Look in detail at one lesson you have taught recently and try to decide what aspects of it drew upon professional artistry.

2. What characteristics ought a quality mentor to have? (Why?)

3. What rationales do you think ought to be the basis of initial teacher education? (Why?)

4. Have you changed or extended your opinions about any of these matters as a result of your reading so far?

Further reading

Carr, D. (1993) 'Questions of competence', *British Journal of Educational Studies*, **41** (3), pp. 253–71.
Eraut, M. (1989) 'Initial teacher training and the NVQ model', in Burke, J. (Ed.) (1989) *Competency-based education and training*. London: Falmer Press, pp.171–85.

55

Fish, D. (1989) *Learning through practice in initial teacher training.* London: Kogan Page, pp.48–85.

Hoyle, E. (1974) 'Professionality, professionalism and the control of teaching', *London Educational Review*, **3** (2), pp.13–18.

Mansfield, B. (1989) 'Competence and standards', in Burke, J. (Ed.) (1989) *Competency-based education and training.* London: Falmer Press, pp.26–38.

Tuxworth, E. (1989) 'Competence based education and training: background and origins', in Burke, J. (Ed.) (1989) *Competency-based education and training.* London: Falmer Press, pp.10–25.

CHAPTER 3

Quality Learning through Practice: Unearthing Meaning from Experience

Introduction: the primacy of practice

Since the late eighties the public and politicians have been going through a phase of denigrating theory, seeing it as 'something outside the practice of teaching' (Stones 1992b, p.279) and of maintaining the importance of practice alone in producing good teachers. Ironically, at the same time, in the health care professions there has been a distinct move towards what seems to be stiffening the practical course with more theory. Both of these reactions are, on the surface, about redressing balances in previous thinking. In fact, however, they are the result of a fundamental lack of basic philosophical understanding about what professional practice involves, and therefore how it might be learnt and how the learner might be assisted.

Stones, drawing on vast experience of working with teachers and student teachers, shows that those who embrace the TR view of professional practice and who argue for the importance of practice alone see learning to teach as learning a craft skill. Here, neophyte teachers learn by observing other teachers, and the procedures consist of a limited circle of trial, error and folk wisdom. As a result, this version of learning on the job is unsystematic and cannot be generalised. Further, the teacher's role is that of passing on information to the student just as they might to pupils. And the lack of an underlying theory about teaching and learning:

> confines any discussion between experienced and beginning teachers to surface activities of teaching.
> (Stones 1992b, p.9)

By contrast, what is offered here is a book which is based upon a belief in the primacy of practice and in the importance of its underlying theory. That is, it takes as its starting point that in learning any aspect of educational practice (both learning to teach and learning to be a mentor) the professional – or student – should *begin* with action. But this is emphatically not the same as saying that learning something practical is achieved *only* by action, neither is it the same as saying that only practice is of any significance and that theory should be set on one side. Indeed, put simply, there is a closer interrelationship between theory and practice than the lay person understands. No action, unless it is the action of a madman (an irrational being), is devoid of theory, for theory involves beliefs, ideas, assumptions, values and everything we do is thus influenced by theory. What may be absent, of course, is *awareness* of such theories. Thus to speak of training teachers only in practical things is a nonsense perpetrated by those who have neither experienced nor considered the matter in depth.

Clearly, as a basic platform for their work, quality mentors in ITE need to know the philosophical arguments for their practices and to have a grasp of the traditions in which they are working. They also need to be up-to-date in the research knowledge about learning to teach and the developments in the field. Over the last twenty years considerable progress has been made in understanding how to enable students to learn to teach, though by no means all is yet understood. Indeed, the excitement of working in this area is that it is an evolving field, where much is still to be learnt. This requires a knowledge of present levels of understanding, as a sound base for further development, and an enjoyment of working at the edge of the unknown. It also requires a tolerance of uncertainty. Further, mentors may well find that they need to explain these ideas and procedures and discuss them with students, colleagues and clients (parents, governors, etc.). The following pages therefore seek to look in some detail at some of the supporting philosophies, principles, processes and traditions of ITE via two major issues: (i) what is involved in learning something practical; and (ii) what is involved in learning professional practice. Finally, by implication from these two, mentors will be asked to consider what can be said so far about how such learning might be fostered and assisted.

I believe, as Russell also argues, that an attempt to come to grips with the details of how we learn through practice is a much neglected and yet vital aspect of ITE, and therefore of mentoring. Talking of students who are trying to learn how to learn from experience, he makes the point that:

because neither teacher nor tutor has experienced a practicum that concentrated on learning from experience, they have no appropriate images and models to support such purposes.
(Russell 1993a, p.208)

The very next section uses practical work that I often include in mentoring workshops in an attempt to tackle this issue.

(i)

Learning something practical

Quality mentoring, then, involves a detailed understanding and appreciation of how we learn new practice and therefore how the learner can be supported in doing so. The implications of this for professional practice are set out in the second main section of this chapter. In order to gain full insight from that part of the chapter, readers will need first of all to try out a new piece of practice following the instructions in the 'Points for Action' below. Being willing to experience and investigate one's own practice (even a very simple piece of practice) is a vital base from which to work with students. Anyone not interested in working at their own practice in this way would be advised to consider carefully exactly what it is they as mentors have to offer student teachers.

For the purpose of the rest of this chapter I shall take learning to teach as a version (a *professional* version) of practical problem-solving – that is as an activity in which one can only make progress by doing and at the same time being aware of one's actions and how they interact with events, and by simultaneously adjusting those actions in order to discover and/or achieve one's goal. It is also something that can be learnt only by doing it first, because the learning and the knowing-how comes, first of all, as a result of doing. The knowing is, in that sense, in the doing. But learning to become proficient in *professional* activity, because it involves an important moral dimension, involves more than the practice alone. It involves gaining insight into that practice by means of investigating it, reflecting upon it, theorising about it and challenging it with theory from other perspectives (from formal theory or the thinking of others) and considering its moral significance and implications, in order to improve future practice.

TASK 3.1: POINTS FOR ACTION[1]

The task described below is solvable. Most adults take approximately twenty minutes. (Children often take less.) You need no resources except three friends and a place to stand in a line. Please do not write anything down as this would change the nature of the problem.

1. Find three other people to work with (children — of age nine or above — or non-teaching friends are quite appropriate if you can't find colleagues). Stand in a straight line side by side.

2. Each choose a different, single-syllable sound which you can make on a number of occasions. That sound is yours. It will be used to identify you. Be sure that you each choose a different one. Never let anyone else use yours.

3. Starting from one end of your line, each in turn make your sound. This will produce a pattern of sounds. Try it several times always starting from the same end of the line and always following on in the same order.

4. The people on each end of the line should now change place *with the person next to them*. The inner two will now be on the ends. (This is called 'twiddle the ends'.)
    When you have done this, make your own sound, still starting from the same end and following along in order as before. This will produce a new pattern of sounds.

5. Now the two (new) people in the middle should change places, those on the ends staying where they are. (This is called 'twiddle the middle'.) When you have made the move, again make the new pattern of sounds, starting from the same end as always and each person still making the sound they first chose. This will produce a new pattern of sounds.

6. Continue in the following sequence: twiddle the ends and make the new pattern of sounds keeping the sound you first chose and starting as ever from whoever is at the original end of the line; then twiddle the middle and make the new pattern of sound, again starting with the person at the end of the line.

1. I am sharply aware that learning *professional* practice involves problems whose solution is never so clear-cut as that of the task below and that there is a danger in pressing my example too far. However it is as yet the best vehicle I have found for unearthing a number of important issues.

7. Continue to do this, making each move in turn followed immediately by each new pattern of sound, until you come to an appropriate stopping place. (You will know when to stop.)

8. Return to your very first places.

9. The challenge is to produce the ever-changing pattern of sounds made as if you had moved following the rules above, but continuing to stand only in your original place.

Summary of the rules: keep to your own sound, don't write anything down 'twiddle the ends' and make the sounds, and 'twiddle the middle' and make the sounds.

HELPFUL HINTS

1. Be *sure* that you are following the instructions. Help each other to do so.

2. Try producing just the first two sequences of sounds without moving from your starting place. This will give you a feel for what is required.

3. Don't be afraid to keep walking it through (going back to the concrete moves).

4. You will only learn to do this by doing it. Talking will not work as a substitute for doing. Return to the text only when you have produced a performance through to the last move.

Unearthing meaning from the experience

If you have had some struggle with the practical task, do not seek to minimise or hide this. Your problems and your emotional (affective) reaction are an important dimension. Being willing to open these issues up and consider them openly is a vital part of working with student teachers. Maynard and Furlong highlight the point well:

> Learning to teach, as we all know but often fail to remember, is a complex, bewildering and sometimes painful task. It involves developing a practical knowledge base, changes in cognition, developing interpersonal skills and also incorporates an affective aspect.
> (Maynard and Furlong 1993, p.69)

T.S. Eliot reminds us in a vivid phrase that it is possible to be involved in an series of actions, but to fail to come to grips with their significance. In 'Dry Salvages' in *Four Quartets* he describes those who: 'had the experience but missed the meaning'. Russell makes the point that, without careful reconsideration, 'experience often leads to ritual knowledge rather than the desired understanding of principles' (Russell 1993a, p.207).

The following comments are aimed at enabling the reader to unearth some meaning from the experience of this new piece of practice, and begin to perceive some of the principles upon which it was based. Thus, unearthing the meaning comes after or at best during the action – never before it (although of course our own basic theories exist all the time, and we take them with us into the action). This means that although one can think about (theorise about) an action before doing it, learning to practice professionally must begin with action. Often the most useful theory and theorising for achieving action comes *during* the action as well as after it. To some extent the piece of action (practical problem) was only a vehicle for enabling us to consider: how students learn practice; what is involved in learning practice; and how mentors can help students to profit from learning the practice of teaching. The issues raised during the period of reflection upon your new practice will include:

- the nature of learning (as a practical problem-solving activity involving people)

- what can be said about ourselves as learners (and what might be true for others)

- the nature of teaching and learning to teach

- the role of teacher in practical professional problem-solving

- issues in theory and practice (the primacy of practice)

- reflection and reflective practice.

Looking back then on the practical experience, and preferably discussing it with a friend, consider first the questions below and read the comments only subsequently.

TASK 3.2: POINTS FOR CONSIDERATION OR DISCUSSION WITH A COLLEAGUE IN CONSIDERING THE ABOVE TASK

1. What do you know *now* that you didn't know before (facts/procedures)?

2. Where did that knowledge come from?

3. How did you crack this problem? (Many problems can't be cracked of course.)

4. By what processes did you learn to do it? (Did you all learn in the same way?)

    ● What exactly have you learnt (about the task, yourself, learning)?

    ● What did you do?

    ● What are the differences between your way of learning and the ways of others?

    ● From whom did you learn to crack it (from 'teacher'/book/ from others)?

    ● From whom were you *willing* to learn? (Whom did you listen to and why?)

    ● How did you feel?

    ● What theories/beliefs were you working to (about yourself/others)?

    ● What theories *underlay* your actions?

    ● Did you experience 'cognitive dissonance' (believing one thing while doing another)?

    ● What are the possible differences between how you learnt and how someone watching you might learn?

Considering learning

Most participants in this task will have discovered, perhaps with some surprise, that they have learnt to do something new, that is, learnt new procedural knowledge (the task), and at the same time that they have learnt some new factual (propositional) knowledge, in the shape of a number of rules that were not given at the start — for example, where to stop in the sequence, and what happens to the people when they get to each end of the row. This is because what they were given was a skeleton framework only, not a series of detailed moves. Most importantly, they will have discovered that they had to oscillate on a number of occasions between returning to the concrete and reworking the physical moves and then trying again to recreate the pattern of sounds at the abstract level. This is an important issue in learning something practical. In learning practical things, not only children but adults also need to go back much more frequently to the concrete than Piaget has led us all to believe. As important is the fact that much of the knowledge involved in cracking the problem has come from the *learner*, and the interaction of one learner with another, and has not been *given* by 'teacher'. And during that interaction there will have been emotional reactions also, which will have affected both who was listened to and how the learning proceeded (usually in fits and starts).

Further, the activity is both an individual activity and also a group one. The more the group was prepared to take risks the more quickly it will have found ways of cracking the problem. Every learner will have learnt differently. Every learner will have uncovered some things about him/herself, about his/her views about how she/he learns, and thus about how other people should learn. Every group attempting to crack the problem will have found their own group way of doing so. Anyone watching rather than doing would have had a very different experience from those participating. Anyone attempting to crack the problem by means of writing would immediately render it a different (non-practical) problem. Anyone attempting to *train* people to produce the end result would again create a very different kind of learning, and a very different meaning would then emerge.

Clearly, then, the only way to learn to do the activity is by doing it. No amount of talking about it renders it any the more achievable. Learning to do depends upon putting action first. And 'doing' here involves concrete doing − trying out various techniques − and thinking critically about them and being willing to drop them if they do not work. In short this is about improvising, reading the situation and rethinking it. And this is happening while participants are on their feet, moving and making sounds all at the same time. As we shall see later, this is what Schön refers to as 'thinking-in-action' and 'knowing-in-action' (see Schön 1987, Chapter 2).

It is also important to note, however, that in considering this activity, some people will argue that a detailed analysis of what has happened during this learning is achievable only up to a point. For them, how the final performance has been achieved is to some extent a mystery. They consider that it is not possible to recreate totally all of the fleeting thoughts and actions in the order in which they happened or to know exactly how certain ideas suddenly emerged. Some, on the other hand, believe that you can atomise the events down to the last single action, plot the moves and then teach them to others. These two extreme views arise from the two polar approaches to professional practice described in Chapter 2 above. The considerable importance of this for trying to understand how students learn the practice of teaching will be considered in the next section of this chapter. Meanwhile, if you wish to pursue further some of these notions about learning you should read Nias (1987). As you do so you should consider the role of formal theory in your present learning.

Let us now turn to the issues about teaching which also lie embedded in the experience. Consider first the following questions which focus upon my role as 'teacher' in setting up this problem and in helping learners to unearth the meaning from it.

TASK 3.3: POINTS FOR CONSIDERATION OR DISCUSSION WITH A COLLEAGUE

1. What have been the various roles of the 'teacher' in this practical problem-solving activity?

2. What might they involve in real practice as opposed to the method I have had to use because this is a book?

3. What were my intentions in setting this problem up for you?

4. What sorts of teaching strategies are involved in using a problem-solving situation?

5. Where does 'authority' reside in the activity?

6. Was it in the same place throughout? (What did you take on trust? What did you challenge?)

Considering teaching

When I offer this activity as part of mentoring workshops, I start by using four volunteers to demonstrate the task. This is because in a workshop everything is done orally and demonstrations help to make the task clear, which is more important when participants have no instructions to refer back to as the reader has here. These demonstrations do *not*, however, offer a model to be followed. They merely offer a picture of the rules. In fact I stop the demonstration before the entire sequence has been revealed. It is an interesting issue to consider exactly what role demonstration plays in learning to teach. This will be taken up in the next new section below.

During the demonstrations and afterwards I work hard to get participants to trust me and to be willing to have a go at the task. This is because they can't yet know about my purpose in using this task as a vehicle to get at issues that lie deeper (and so the task might seem trivial) and because I must set an atmosphere in which it is safe to take risks, to get it wrong, to try again, to profit from mistakes and to see them as growing points. I also have to ensure that everyone has equal rights to their opinions and to their own ways of doing things, in order that everyone will feel safe to learn. I cannot do some of these things so easily via the printed word, but you might like to consider how I have tried to achieve some of them.

It is important to notice the minimal role of instructions in the activity. I said above that what I offered was a mere skeleton of rules. Certainly I offered you nine points and four hints. But I also believed that you would find certain things out for yourselves and in doing so would own them more fully than you would have done had I told you them. The teacher here has to trust the participants to draw upon a range of pre-existing knowledge and to be able to uncover it in order to crack the problem. Such an approach is important too in dealing with student teachers who do not come as blank sheets to the process of becoming a teacher. This means that the teacher who uses practical problem-solving gives up the authority role in order to become an enabler, to set the scene in a supportive way and to encourage the learners to draw upon their own resources. The locus of authority then resides not in the teacher, who, in the workshop version, stands at the back rather than the front during the demonstration, who focusses the class on the demonstrating quartet, who sends fours off to practise privately and who leads the reflections afterwards by means of questions rather than statements. The locus of authority is, rather, with the learners. During practice the group discovers that authority resides in different learners at different points in the process. And the negotiation of this between learners is of considerable interest in terms of group dynamics, since quite often an individual discovers with some horror that they have attempted to take the group over or to impose on someone else a learning style that is inappropriate for them. Quite often, too, a group in difficulties only cracks it when one individual having trouble eventually rejects the dominance of another who has sought to impose one way of learning on everyone, and strikes out for his/her own way of doing it. If you wish to pursue further some of these ideas about teaching, see Passmore (1980). As you do so consider the use of formal theory in your own learning about this.

All of this raises some very interesting issues about theory and practice. The following section seeks to explore this.

Theory and practice
The role of theory in practical affairs is in fact central as was indicated at the beginning of this chapter and, as we see below, as Wilfred Carr and Eraut also point out. For our purposes (for the moment) there are two main kinds of theory. Formal theory is formulated and argued for publicly, is commonly known and generally (if temporarily) accepted as current thinking (which is sometimes mistaken for proven fact). Personal theory is a mixture of beliefs and assumptions, values and private theories (perhaps influenced by formal theory), which cashes out into everyday practice. Carr draws our attention to the elements of formal theory which can influence practice, but notes how in practice it is transmuted by personal theory:

> what is distinctive of an educational practice is that it is guided, not just by some general practical theory, but also by the exigencies of the practical situation in which this theory is to be applied. Thus, the guidance given by theory always has to be moderated by the guidance given by *phronesis* – wise and prudent judgement about if, and to what extent, this 'theory' ought to be invoked and enacted in a concrete case.
> (Carr, W. 1987, pp.172–3)

Eraut focusses on personal theory. He makes the points that when people start using a theory they stop calling it a theory and that people become alienated by 'theory' as a result of being constantly subjected to other peoples' rather than being encouraged to develop (or to recognise) their own. He adds:

> Yet people use theory all the time; and it is their personal theories which determine how they interpret the world and their encounters with people and situations within it.
> (Eraut 1989, p.184)

Within personal theory, Argyris and Schön make a useful distinction between espoused theories (the theories of action to which we give allegiance when asked to say what we believe) and theories-in-use (the theories that actively govern our actions) (see Argyris and Schön 1974, pp. 6−7). This often leads to the difference between knowing what one should do and doing something else. How espoused theories become theories-in-use is an interesting question.

TASK 3.4: POINTS FOR CONSIDERATION OR DISCUSSION WITH A COLLEAGUE

1. What espoused theories did you bring to this practice (about yourself, learning, problem-solving)?

2. What 'theories-in-use' lay under your actions? Did both sets of theories match?

3. How will the experience influence your future practice, your views about theory and your own theories?

Many participants in the above problem-solving exercise realise, on looking back at it, that they had begun the task with a number of theories about, for example, how to solve such problems, how to tackle this particular one, how they could best learn, what the task was really about. In some cases participants will have begun with some theories about how a tutor involved in INSET should operate during a workshop or an author should behave in a book (and therefore how a practising teacher should be expected to learn) and have found these in contrast to the practice associated with this task. The reader may even have felt surprise as I flouted some of the conventions of writing a book by sending the audience away from the text to carry out some practice. As Schön points out, surprise is a useful signal to attend to in trying to explore and improve practice. It often draws attention to the unexpected, and this in turn often marks the existence of a conflict between belief and action (a challenge to practice by theory or vice versa) (see Schön 1987, pp.26−8).

During the trial and error of the activity, no doubt assorted theories conflicted internally within individuals and no doubt externally between group members, and probably theory was modified by practice and vice versa. While all of these theories-in-action are held fluidly, while theory is remembered to consist of unproven ideas and while participants are willing to adjust their ideas and their practices according to the needs of the specific situation, both theory and practice can refine each other. Eraut, who looks at the problems of specifying teaching in TR terms, refers to the importance of 'flexibility, adaptability, situational understanding and ability to learn from experience'. He also makes the point (quoting Nisbett and Ross 1980) that: 'there is a considerable body of psychological evidence to show that personal theories have a significant effect on how people think, act and perform' (see Eraut 1989, p.184). And this is all true both for the learners and for the teacher.

Recognising the theories which underlie our work provides us with the power to 'bring the largely intuitive aspects of . . . practice under some kind of critical control'. He adds, significantly:

> Once one becomes more aware of the nature and effect of one's own theories, then it is possible to also consider those of others, whether they be immediate colleagues or authors of books. Similarly, by recognising the contexts in which one has developed one's theories, one is better able to judge when new theories are needed to cope with new kinds of contexts.
> (Eraut 1989, p.184)

Eraut also highlights the role of theory in strategic thinking, which requires an understanding of the context, a set of priorities, awareness of alternatives and an ability to predict the consequences of various courses of action over the longer term. Participants in the set task may see, on looking back over it, that they did indeed draw upon these and as a result did initiate or abort particular attempts at action. But it is in fact very difficult to 'see' or to trace such happenings by observation unless it enters the discussion between group members and that discussion is recorded.

All of this strongly challenges the notion of the mentor (or HEI tutor) simply telling a student how to teach or what to do in a classroom. And it is why the DES publication which speaks of 'giving the student the skills' of teaching (see above, p.17) was so horrifying to those who were really knowledgeable in this area. Finally, then, it remains to ask some questions about reflective practice and the processes of reflection. McIntyre argues that reflection is a subset of theorising (see McIntyre 1993, p.43). It could also be argued that reflection is a tool of investigation. Such issues are taken up in Chapter 6 below. It is first necessary to clarify the ideas involved and to relate them to the task given above.

TASK 3.5: POINTS FOR CONSIDERATION OR DISCUSSION WITH A COLLEAGUE

1. List briefly the things you have learnt as a result of the reflections prompted above.

2. How have these reflections affected your understanding of the experience of the task?

3. What do you understand by reflection on practice and what processes are involved in it?

4. How might what you have learnt through practice today relate to your later professional practice?

Reflective practice

All of the activities and discussions in the three subsections above have been versions of or approaches to reflection on practice. Without such processes, the meaning and significance of the task would probably have lain dormant in the minds of readers and thus never impacted upon future practice. For this reason, reflection is, for those who subscribe to the PA view, a central tool in learning through practice. For those whose mentoring is guided by a TR approach, of course, telling and training are what matter. My argument, however, is that that approach may make for short-term efficiency, but that it deprives learners of individuality and of the means of developing and improving their practice in the longer term.

Reflection itself is about reconsidering – even 're-seeing' practice. It is located within the tradition of experiential learning (see Osterman and Kottkamp 1993, p.20) and can happen both during and after the action. (There can be consideration of action beforehand which also involves some imagined viewing of what is intended or some reconsideration of previous practice.) Reflection may involve a number of processes. There is no simple set pattern for this – that is one of its strengths (though it often involves the four elements of Kolb's experiential learning theory: concrete experience; observation and analysis (or interpretation); abstract reconceptualisation; and active experimentation). (See Kolb 1984, and Osterman and Kottkamp 1993, p.20.) What can be said, however, is that any systematic approach to reflection can be used to investigate and theorise about practice. The process of reflection enables critical consideration of practice and its moral dimensions. This does presuppose a seeking rather than a knowing attitude to practice and to one's responsibilities within practice, and thus it requires the practitioner to be open to criticism and to the possible need to change. What it does not do is to provide a clear set of detailed instructions for carrying out new practice. In that it is tentative and enquiring rather than assertive about knowledge, reflection is very much against the prevailing climate of our (rather unintelligent) times, where certainty of intention and achievement and simplicity of skills and procedures seem to be expected in every occupation irrespective of the nature of that occupation.

Reflective practice, then, is about using reflection to enlighten, develop and improve professional action. It is 'an empowering and motivational process' which enables individuals to be more effective and assume greater responsibility for their own practices (Osterman and Kottkamp 1993, p.185) and it takes both practice and theory seriously (see Golby 1993a, p.41).

Schön has provided us with some important (if controversial and incomplete) notions and some useful language in which to distinguish two different kinds of reflection. These he calls reflection-in-action and reflection-on-action. He relates the first of these to what he calls **knowing-in-action**. By this he means the kinds of knowledge we show in our intelligent action. He cites as examples public, observable actions like riding a bicycle and private actions like analysing a balance sheet. In both cases he maintains, the knowing is *in* the action. And we show the existence of such knowing through our spontaneous, skilful carrying out of the performance. The processes involved in such knowing-in-action, however, often cannot be made verbally explicit but can sometimes be observed or reflected upon afterwards in order to describe the tacit knowing embedded in them. For example, we can uncover the sequences of our procedures and processes and the rules we follow, as well as our values, beliefs and personal theories, all of which are given away by overt clues. Schön argues that:

> whatever language we employ, however, our descriptions of knowing-in-action are always *constructions*. They are always attempts to put into explicit, symbolic form a kind of intelligence that begins by being tacit and spontaneous. Our descriptions are conjectures that need to be tested against observations of their originals – which, in at least one respect, they are bound to distort. For knowing-in-action is dynamic, and 'facts', 'procedures', 'rules', and 'theories' are static.
> (Schön 1987, p.25)

Schön goes on to explain how in response to the jolt of the unexpected during a piece of action, we may reflect upon the incident by looking back upon it, or we may pause in the midst of action (but momentarily outside it) to think what we should do next (Schön 1987, pp.27−31). These are both examples of **reflection-on-action**, in which we relate (to a piece of practice we have recently executed), some ordered, deliberate and systematic questions about practice, which arise specifically *from* that practice. There is no set version of this and reflection can utilise a range of different processes, chosen for their appropriateness to the specific piece of practice. Without much conscious experience of this process, however, practitioners are inclined to reflect in a totally haphazard way, seizing on any aspect of the practice that first comes to mind. Readers may have done this in moments when they stopped their actions in the given task and discussed what to do next. For this reason a systematic approach to reflection is needed. But it must be one which allows the user to be responsive to the specific and unique characteristics of the activity under consideration. A flexible framework rather than a set of routines is therefore needed. One such is offered and considered in detail in Chapter 6 below.

Of reflection-in-action, on the other hand, Schön says:

> When we have learned how to do something, we can execute smooth sequences of activity, recognition, decision, and adjustment without having, as we say, to 'think about it'.
> (Schön 1987, p.26)

(Readers may not have reached that stage with the task set above, but if they practised it for long enough it would happen.) Schön goes on:

> Our spontaneous knowing-in-action usually gets us through the day. On occasion, however, it doesn't. A familiar routine produces an unexpected result; an error stubbornly resists correction ... All such experiences ... contain an element of *surprise*.
> (Schön 1987, p.26)

Then, we may reflect in the middle of the action (while we can still make a difference to the action we are involved in and *without interrupting it*). This is reflection-in-action. In this case, and simultaneously with continuing the action, we perceive a puzzle and invent and implement solutions, using on-the-spot experimentation and trial and error which is not random and which involves critical questioning of the assumptions and structure of knowing-in-action. This process includes restructuring both our strategies and also our very thinking about and our understanding of the action. Schön talks here of 'ways of re-framing problems'. (Readers will probably have experienced such processes during the set task.) Reflection-in-action, then, has immediate significance for action and is even coincidental with it. Schön maintains that a skilled performer can adjust his responses to variations which occur moment by moment, and integrate reflection-in-action into a smooth performance of an on-going task.

Russell and Munby, who have worked on Schön's ideas for ten years, characterise reflection-in-action as 'a process with nonlogical features that is prompted by experience and over which we have limited control' (Russell and Munby 1991, p.164). For them 'the essence of reflection-in-action is 're-framing' (Schön's term) which means the 'hearing' or 'seeing' differently in which observation is interpretative rather than analytical. Reframing, they say, 'mediates between theory and practice, revealing new meanings in theory and new strategies for practice' (Russell and Munby 1991, p.166). Though they add that a new frame does not mean an end to puzzles and problems, but rather, the 'scrutiny of one's own practice continues, but moves on to more elaborated views of practice' (Russell and Munby 1991, p.173).

Their research so far has led them to view the reframing of puzzling experiences, particularly those about the inconsistency of theory and practice, as very significant in developing teachers' professional knowledge and action. They also note that revised theories-in-action are accompanied by changes in the teachers' descriptive language.

> Seeking consistency between theory and practice and better theories to guide practice appears to be an important element in productive reframing.
> (Russell and Munby 1991, p.184)

Schön himself translates all of this into a professional context, discussing professional practice in the terms of a practical problem like making a gate (Schön 1987, Chapter 2). We shall pick up on his fourth notion − that of knowing-in-practice (where practice refers to professional practice as a whole) − in the section below.

TASK 3.6: POINTS FOR CONSIDERATION OR DISCUSSION WITH A COLLEAGUE

So far we have discussed the practical task given at the start of this chapter under the headings 'learning', 'teaching', 'theory and practice' and 'reflecting on practice'.

1. Review in your mind what you have learnt about each of these four.

2. List briefly the implications of the given task and these discussions of it for *learning to teach*.

3. You may like to compare your list with that which comes towards the end of the next section.

(ii)

Learning professional practice

So far we have considered a practical problem-solving task which can be solved. This task, though a practical one, is not strictly a professional one, though it is closely related to the nature of professional practice in its requirement for collaborative learning and in that it can be learnt only by doing. Some of the main differences, however, between it and a professional activity aimed at learning to teach are:

1 that the task was an individual 'one-off' activity

2. that the set task was susceptible to solution

3. that, although the means by which people learn to do it are variable, the solution (final performance) has the same surface features for everyone, everywhere

4. that there is nothing contestable about the solution, which receives universal agreement

5. that there are no moral complexities about the solution.

By contrast, solutions to individual activities in professional practice are best understood from within that tradition, are at best temporary (can never be fully solved), are situation specific, are essentially contestable (because value-related), and have a moral dimension. Indeed, learning to teach is an open capacity, cannot be mastered and goes on being refined for ever. (Arguably there is a major onus on mentors to demonstrate this and to reveal its implications in their practice.)

As Michael Golby points out, in the term 'professional practice' the word 'practice' refers not to an individual activity but to a 'whole tradition in which particular activities are related together as part of a social project or mission' (Golby 1993a, p.4). For education, the social project is the promotion of knowledge, just as for the legal profession it is justice and for the medical profession it is health. He also makes the point that this enterprise of teaching is not value-free (see also Chapter 1 above). Values, as he points out, though they underlie the daily activities of practitioners, are not delivered as end products. 'Discussion of values and principles is therefore best conducted in the context of specific professional activities'. He goes on to make the point that professional practice:

> is not merely habitual skilled behaviour but a stream of highly mis-cellaneous activities unified as serving a social good. Practice has a history which can be seen as the collective pursuit of human good; as an historic phenomenon, practices have their own language and style. Though there are of necessity routine and unreflecting parts of daily professional life, loss of sight of fundamental values which have evolved historically in the activities of practice is at once a loss of professionalism.
> (Golby 1993a, p.5)

He also offers us the important understanding that just as the unique speaking of an individual relies upon the pre-existence of our own language (which comes to us as received tradition of expression, carrying cultural traditions), so 'educational practice has its own history and culture in which individual practitioners participate' and which they express in their own way. Thus, learning to become a professional is 'a matter of coming ever more fully into membership of a tradition of practice' and 'at its maturity it is a matter of taking part in more fully shaping practice for the future'. This involves understanding the inherited traditions of a profession (and/or of the preparation to enter that profession) and considering critically and practically their present relevance (see Golby 1993a, p.8).

We therefore need to consider what can now be said about the processes of learning professional practice and exactly what we can draw from our discussions of the set task to enlighten our understanding of learning professional practice and of enabling others to learn it.

The philosophical bases of learning professional practice

The nature of professional practice, then, is social, moral and complex and is embedded in traditions of practice. The ability to teach cannot be mastered. We can already say that learning professional practice is achieved by learning through experience. What can we say then about this idea and its history?

The notion of learning through experience goes back to the Greeks, where it was shaped by Aristotle's notions of 'praxis', and comes to us more immediately via Dewey, Van Mannen, Schwab, Stenhouse and Schön. These are the thinkers who have shaped the traditions which mentors are now adopting.

Wilfred Carr, with reference to Aristotle, points out that 'the classical concept of practice ... has always exercised a decisive influence on education' and that although the Greek word '*praxis*' means roughly the same as our term 'practice', the classical context in which it existed gave it a different dimension. Thus *praxis* is a way of distinguishing 'doing something' from *poesis*, 'making something'. The end of *poesis* is an object which is known prior to the action, and the processes involved in this production are guided by a form of knowledge which Aristotle calls *techne* – which we would now call technical knowledge. *Poesis* is a species of rule-following action. Carr reminds us that for Aristotle the activities of shipbuilders, craftsmen and artisans were paradigm cases of *poesis* guided by *techne*. *Praxis* is also directed to the achievement of an end, not a concrete end but the end of 'some morally worthwhile good'. Such good cannot be made. It can only be done. Practice is thus a form of 'doing (moral) action', whose end can be realised only through action and can exist only in action. These ends are not immutable and fixed. They cannot be specified in advance of the action. They are what they are at the time and can be understood only in terms of the tradition in which the good intrinsic to practice is enshrined. He says that a practice:

> is always the achievement of a tradition, and it is only by sub-mitting to its authority that practitioners can begin to acquire the practical knowledge and standards of excellence by means of which their own practical competence can be judged. But the authoritative nature of a tradition does not make it immune to criticism. The practical knowledge made available through tradition is not simply reproduced; it is also constantly re-interpreted and revised through dialogue and discussion about how to pursue the practical goods which constitute the tradition.
>
> (Carr, W. 1987, pp.169–70)

Thus, he argues, by a process of a critical reconstruction, the tradition evolves and changes.

Dewey is the modern philosopher whose ideas about learning through experience have provided the foundations for practical-based education in the twentieth century. It is in highlighting the fact that professional practice is the province of a community of practitioners who share the traditions of a calling that part of Dewey's contribution to our thinking is made. He also offers us perspectives on the knowledge needed and the processes involved in learning through practice. He it was who first discussed reflective practice and distinguished between routine (unthinking) actions and reflective actions which show awareness of the principles and grounds of our practices. He also pointed out that systematic enquiry into practice is necessary to bring this fully to consciousness, in order that we have a secure understanding of the grounds of our actions (see Dewey 1933).

Van Manen's work is important in offering an early model of reflection. His view of reflection is hierarchical. He suggests three levels of reflection: the first being concerned with technical practical details; the second with assumptions that underlie action and the worth of competing educational goals; and the third with moral and ethical issues (see Van Manen 1990, in which he reiterates his original contribution). He is critical of action research that simply slips from reflection-on-action straight to problem-solving, and emphasises the second and third levels of reflection as essential.

Schwab has developed our ideas in respect of deliberation, which is a kind of public and social form of reflection aimed particularly at decision-making about curriculum design and evaluation (see Schwab 1969).

Stenhouse developed the important notion of the teacher as researcher (Stenhouse 1975), now developed further into the idea of enquiring teacher by the work of, for example, Elliott, Hopkins, Nias and Rudduck. He argued for the 'emancipation' of teachers by encouraging them to adopt the perspective of researchers. The process of being a teacher-researcher (or of making teaching enquiry-based) would, he believed, strengthen teacher judgement and lead to the self-directed improvement of practice. Accordingly, his many and powerful writings about research, published between the late 1970s and, posthumously, the mid-1980s (focussing, for example, on what counts as research, the role of research in teaching, the case-study tradition), have provided an important basis for helping reflective teachers to investigate their practice (see Rudduck and Hopkins 1985, p.3). For him the means to professional development for teachers was a research process in which they systematically reflected on their practice and used the results to improve their teaching (see the notion of taking an investigative stance towards teaching in Chapter 4 below). In Carr's words, Stenhouse related 'the idea of "teacher as researcher" to an analysis of professionalism' (see Carr, W. 1989, p.7). Stenhouse also subscribed to the notion of teaching as an art in which 'ideas and action are fused' in the practice of one's own performance. Comparing the art of teaching with artistry generally he wrote of the development of art as 'a dialectic of ideas and practice not to be separated from change'. He added of art:

> Exploration and interpretation lead to revision and adjustment of idea and of practice ... look at the sketchbook of a good artist, a play in rehearsal, a jazz quartet working together. That, I am arguing, is what good teaching is like ...
> Note, however, that the process of developing the art of the artist is always associated with change in ideas and practice ... There is no mastery, always aspiration. And the aspiration is about ideas — content, as well as about performance — execution of ideas.
> (Stenhouse, in Rudduck and Hopkins 1985, p.97)

Schön extends these ideas about teaching as an art, considering matters like improvisation and its role in teaching. But most importantly he has analysed technical rationality and found it wanting on three counts (see Schön 1983 and 1987):

1. It ignores the extent to which professional knowledge is and must be exercised in the institutional settings particular to the profession.

2. It is indifferent to the way professionals actually work.

3. It underrates the messy complexity of practice.

Most importantly, though, and because he rejects the TR approach, Schön has contributed to our development of an epistemology of practice and to our developing language of reflection.

> If the model of Technical Rationality ... fails to account for practical competence in divergent situations, so much the worse for the model. Let us search instead for an epistemology of practice implicit in artistic, intuitive processes which some practitioners do bring to situations of uncertainty, instability, uniqueness and value conflict.
> (Schön 1983, p.49)

We have already looked at some of Schön's central concepts in his theory of knowledge of practice and shall consider more below. Before moving to these, however, we should note that Schön's work is a beginning not an end. He has begun a process which needs much more work before we have a full sense of how knowing-in-practice operates, and even then we shall not have been able to analyse it absolutely nor shall we have mastered it. What Schön offers, then, is ideas on which practitioners need to work. However, there are a number of critics of his work – who view teaching in a more TR way. For example, Gilroy is unhappy about the varying uses of the term 'reflection' and what he sees as the unhelpfulness of uncertainty. He (rightly in my view) sees the possibilities of infinite regression in an undisciplined version of reflection which omits discussion of wider issues, including moral aspects, and which ignores the contribution to thinking of the views and ideas of others (see Gilroy 1993). Gilroy supports the work of Stones and sees teaching as a game in which the rules should be defined. (This raises interesting questions not only about what such rules consist of and how to gain consensus for all but the most general, but also about whether artistry involves playing creatively within rules or finding creative expression that goes beyond them. It is thus not clear how far this analogy can be taken.) Hartley (1993) also sees reflective practice as undesirable in that it often operates only at a descriptive level. However, like Gilroy's reservations, his are not about the work of Schön, but about the problems that occur when it is misused.

TASK 3.7: POINTS FOR CONSIDERATION OR DISCUSSION WITH A COLLEAGUE

1. Review in your mind what you have learnt from the brief history of ideas offered in this subsection.

2. How do they relate to those offered in Chapter 2 above?

Some key concepts in learning professional practice

Learning professional practice, then, though complex and never entirely able to be analysed, clearly involves learning through experience. There are a number of concepts associated with this, which have been usefully elucidated by Schön (1983 and 1987), and some of them have been explored further by Russell (see Russell 1993a).

Schön has highlighted knowing-in-action, reflection-in-action and reflection-on-action, and he has called attention to the importance of puzzles and surprises and to the notion of 'reframing'. In learning practice Schön's idea of a **sheltered practicum** is also useful. (This is an experience of practice where the student has a taste of real practice but does not bear the full responsibility for every aspect of the work.) Schön describes the main features of a practicum as: 'learning by doing, coaching rather than teaching, and a dialogue of reciprocal reflection-in-action between coach and student' (see Schön 1987, p.303; see pp.86–7 for his ideas on coaching).

Russell explores the processes of learning through experience as they are related to learning to teach. He makes the point that because in ITE we have lacked detail about how student teachers can learn through experience, practices developed on teaching practice 'easily become rituals without supporting principles, and theory, often seen as elaborate common sense, is comprehended but not related to practices' (Russell 1993a, p.209). He traces the problem to the fact that direct experience can lead to ritual knowledge without principled understanding, because the learner's understanding of practice remains 'at the level of specific experiences and practical procedures'. Drawing on the work of Edwards and Mercer (1987), which looks at children's learning through experience, Russell highlights the usefulness for ITE of their notions of **ritual knowledge** (routinised know-how) and **principled knowledge**. Russell describes their concept of 'principled knowledge' as: 'essentially explanatory, oriented towards understanding of how procedures and processes work, of why certain conclusions are necessary or valid rather than being arbitrary things to say because they seem to please the teacher'. Russell makes the point that: 'changing one's patterns, particularly in the light of theory or research, requires knowledge of the principles implicit in the present practices, and here ritual knowledge is inadequate' (see Russell 1993a, p.210). He goes on to argue that at present most teachers' practical knowledge remains ritualised and that there are no traditions of using the observation and analysis of working teachers to enable them to move from ritual to principles. He points out that normally observation of a professional teacher is used only when they are already failing, and concludes:

> Observation of teachers by those with more experience and authority competes directly with the potential of experience to modify teachers'

frames for conducting and interpreting their work. So long as teachers associate observation with the threat of potentially arbitrary criticism, the profession denies itself opportunity to discover the value of recording teaching events for subsequent review and detailed analysis, leading to understanding of the principles implicit in present practices.
(Russell 1993a, p.214)

We thus have a range of useful concepts related to learning professional practice. To these might be added the following crucial distinctions:

- learning professional practice (which means learning to operate within a tradition)

- learning from practice (which means learning by watching and perhaps copying)

- learning by practice (which means learning by endless repeating of actions)

- learning through practice (which means learning about principled actions via the learning of one specific activity).

This last version is about establishing the foundation of principled procedures, and is important because learning to bring practice under control and improve it is aided by exhuming and examining the principles underlying our actions (see Fish 1989, Chapter 4).

All of this has a number of things to tell us about how to learn to teach and how to enable students to learn to teach. It also offers us critical perspectives on present models of learning professional practice.

Some models of learning professional practice

There are many models proposed that purport to exemplify how professional practice might be acquired and improved. They all have the universal drawback of models in that they reduce and simplify the complexity of practice. But some offer us useful ideas – even if they are ideas that we reject – because they help us to clarify our thinking. The following outlines some of the better known ideas which are currently influencing thinking about ITE.

TASK 3.8: POINTS FOR CONSIDERATION OR DISCUSSION WITH A COLLEAGUE

It is instructive to ask of each model as you read, what are its underlying views about:

- the character of teaching

- students as learners

- the capabilities of teachers as mentors/reflective practitioners

- how students and mentor-teachers will relate together.

Some models were originally devised to structure learning in other professions and have been taken over by those who are designing ITE courses. These are all based upon TR notions of incremental approaches to learning practice. They assume that learners can operate only at a simple (noviciate) level in all early practice and become more dependable experts the more practice they have. Such models include that of Benner (1984), in nursing, who suggests that student nurses climb gradually through a range of competences from novice to expert, and whose work was based upon the skill acquisition model of Dreyfus and Dreyfus (1986). This influential model offers a five stage progression from novice to expert which was developed in the context of the training of aircraft pilots. Both Dreyfus and Dreyfus and Benner posit that capturing the descriptions of expert practice is important, and is possible, though difficult, because the expert 'operates from a deep understanding of the total situation' (Benner 1984, p.32). Though apparently less than fully TR, these models run contrary to the notion of PA which sees students as bringing knowledge with them, finding it in action and as being able to consider some moral dimensions of practice and deal with incidents in practice with a wisdom that is not necessarily related to length of practice.

Even models developed with student teachers in mind are often incrementally shaped, and TR in character, being influenced by the idea that teaching can be atomised into all of its individual components. They chase the chimera of seeking either generalisations that can be taught to student-teachers or *the* definitive structure for course design. Of note here is the work of Eraut (1989), whose three-dimensional performance model attempts to map the contexts, conditions and situations of individual performances in order to chart competences of teaching. In this spirit too (although Harvard and Dunne (1992) reject this categorisation) is the work of Dunne *et al.* at Exeter which is concerned with levels of pedagogic reasoning and which is informed by Vygotsky's model of cognitive development through social interaction (see Bennett and Carré 1993, for details of this work).

Arguably the most persuasive of work towards this sort of model is that of Brown and McIntyre 1993. They have tried to gain access to teachers' professional craft knowledge. They sought to look at what good teachers do and how they discuss it (what concepts they employ); that is, to 'illuminate the ways in which teachers themselves construe what they are doing and to assess the extent to which there are generalizations to be made across teachers' (Brown and McIntyre 1993, p.17). What they have to report about teachers' actions and their discussion of them is interesting and useful. The drive to seek generalisations from this to use to train student teachers might however lead it to be used in a TR way.

The work of McIntyre and Haggar at Oxford illustrates this. They are developing models of learning to teach which are predicated on the notion that students learn the craft skills of teaching in a first phase of learning to teach and only later, towards the end of their course, learn to reflect upon practice. McIntyre sees reflection as 'a circumscribed sub-category of theorising' (lecture given by McIntyre at the Cambridge mentoring conference in March 1994) and argues that there is a limited role for reflection in initial training and that it is rarely practised even amongst experienced teachers. He proposes three levels of reflection: the technical, the practical and the critical (thus assuming a hierarchy and echoing the work of Van Manen). He sees the earliest (technical) stage as when students are concerned with achieving given goals, the second stage being when they are articulating their own criteria and evaluating their own practice and the third when they are concerned with the wider ethical and social/political issues.

By contrast, the work of Furlong and Maynard at Swansea is aimed at developing a model of how students learn. In 1988, Furlong *et al.* argued for what Furlong later admits was an over-hierarchical set of four levels of professional training (Maynard and Furlong 1993). More recently they have been working on the way students develop and on the levels of learning, and thus of mentoring, that they go through. This still seems to be a hierarchical view of learning and to accept an incremental, rather than embracing a holistic, view of learning to teach. They seem to see the student's learning to teach as moving from an apprentice form, through a learning of simple strategies, to reflection and on to attainment of autonomy. This involves associated changes in role for the mentor, who acts initially as model for the student and later becomes a critical friend and a partner in teaching some lessons (lecture given by Furlong at the Cambridge mentoring conference (March 1994)).

We are now in a position to summarise what we might say so far about the processes through which professional practice of teaching is learnt and to distinguish the issues central to that learning.

Issues and processes useful in learning to teach

It is, of course, possible to say only some tentative things about learning to teach at this stage. But even these probably represent progress in our understanding compared to what it was at the start of the book.

TASK 3.9: POINTS FOR CONSIDERATION OR DISCUSSION WITH A COLLEAGUE

Readers are invited:

- to consider critically the following list of points

- to compare these with their own, made in response to the task on page 49

- to reconsider the views that underlay their early responses to the exercises in Chapter 1 (pp.30–1)

The following summarises some points useful in understanding how we learn to teach.

- Action comes first.

- Action has theories embedded in it because theory and practice are part of each other.

- Theory comes in a variety of forms, including personal theory and formal theory.

- Personal theory includes espoused theory and theories-in-use.

- Learners come with knowledge already which needs to be explored and built upon.

- Learners often need the minimum enabling framework to start with.

- There is a need to return to the concrete frequently and to oscillate between this and principles relevant to the practice (to engage in a 'dialectic of ideas and practice', in Stenhouse's terms).

- It is quite possible to move bodily, make sounds and think *at the same time*.

- Such 'thoughtful action' (which Schön calls knowing-in-action) often involves improvising and thinking on one's feet.

- Insight into action can then be gained by reflecting on, theorising about and investigating practice.

- Gaining insight means unearthing the meaning, and thus the significant values and the principles, beneath the actions.

- To this extent any one piece of action is a vehicle for learning principles.

- Gaining insight into one's own actions is more important than being told by someone else what to do and how.

- Practical learning proceeds in fits and starts.

- There is a strong affective element.

- Every learner will learn differently.

- Risk-taking is a key to successful practical problem-solving and to the more temporary problem-solving of professional practice.

- Talking, reading or writing about the task is no substitute for the experience of doing it (though it can aid reflection-on-action afterwards).

- Being trained to do something practical is a quite different process with very different and less-transferable outcomes.

- The role of demonstration in learning practice need not be the same as apprenticeship. Demonstration can be used to set the problem, not show how to solve it.

- It is important to set an atmosphere where risks can be taken, mistakes made and where everyone has equal say.

- Practice needs to be observed, captured and used to work towards its informing principles.

- Reflection on practice may not lead to immediate visible improvement, but rather to longer-term quality in practice and professionalism.

The final question, then, is: what does this tell us about the skills, processes and issues necessary for a mentor to enable students to learn through practice?

Issues and processes useful in mentoring a student teacher

Basically a mentor is someone who enables a student to learn through practice. So far, then, we can say the following kinds of things about the skills and knowledge a mentor needs for this enterprise.

- The locus of knowledge for succeeding in the situation is in the student learner, not in the mentor-teacher.

- In order to enable the student to learn through practice, the mentor has to give up authority, and know how to hand it over to the student.

- The mentor must know how to reflect on practice, know how to investigate practice, know the role of puzzles in learning, and how theory and practice refine each other.

- The mentor must be willing to demonstrate that his/her own practice is developed and refined by these approaches.

- The mentor needs to be a seeker rather than a knower about teaching and learning, and to be comfortable enough with uncertainty to be able to share it with students.

- The mentor needs to be open to criticism and change.

This list might usefully be extended by reference to that of McIntyre and Haggar (1993, pp.91−3). They make the point that the case for teacher-mentors as opposed to tutor supervisors is only a strong one if mentors develop high-level supervisory skills. In summary, they argue that effective supervision depends on mentors (see McIntyre and Haggar 1993, pp.91–3):

- helping the student with planning as well as in teaching
- helping the student to learn from the successes and failures of their practice
- focussing students on the competences required and enabling them to develop their own agendas
- enabling students to learn not only from their strengths but also from their problems
- on each occasion of working with a student, focussing on specific predetermined aspects of teaching, but also responding to other major issues as they arise
- enabling students to recognise successful strategies but persuading them to learn others
- helping students to test the adequacy of their practices and to make explicit their criteria for this
- enabling students to learn the skills, understandings and attitudes to continue their own professional development
- helping them to learn, but also taking responsibility for assessing them – and, where necessary, judging them inadequate.

The literature of mentoring and of ITE is full of articles proposing various models of mentoring (Dunne 1993; Fish 1989; Maynard and Furlong 1993; McIntyre and Haggar 1993) and in the end many are simply formulations of fairly obvious approaches to supervision, though there is also work being carried out on the distinctions between supervision and mentoring (see Wilkin 1992b).

However, it is Schön who offers one of the most useful perspectives on mentor behaviour in his models of coaching. He describes the coach's skill as operating in one of three models, which he emphasises are ideal types and may in reality occur in one session. These models are: 'Joint Experimentation', 'Follow Me' and 'Hall of Mirrors'. Within each model the dialogue of coach and student calls for different sorts of improvisation, presents different orders of difficulty and lends itself to different contexts.

Joint Experimentation is useful when the student already knows what she/he wants to produce. Here the coach first helps the student to formulate the qualities she/he wants to achieve and then by demonstration or description explores different ways of producing them. The skills here involve leading the student to search for ways of operating; the student has to be willing to have a go. The coach 'works at creating and sustaining a process of collaborative enquiry', and must resist the temptation to tell the student how to do it – though she/he can perhaps generate a number of solutions and enable the student to choose (Schön 1987, p.296).

When the coach wants to offer a new way of seeing and doing things, the **Follow Me** approach is apparently more useful. Here the coach improvises 'a whole designlike performance' and offers examples of reflection-in-action. The coach is able to take a holistic view of the action, to break it up into various aspects and to reassemble it. The coach demonstrates and then responds to the student's attempts to imitate him/her. There is danger of confusion and ambiguity, so the coach uses all kinds of language and analogies and the student tries to follow these, attempting to construct her/his own meanings (see Schön 1987, p.296). In its pure form, this model is less useful for working with student teachers than for coaching in other professions, but in its indication of ways of helping students to reflect, it is important, and its spirit is caught by the framework for reflection offered in Chapter 6 below.

In **Hall of Mirrors** 'student and coach continually shift perspective' (see Schön 1987, p.297). They shift from re-enacting the student's practice to dialogue about it, to redesigning it. Here there is 'a premium on the coach's ability to surface his own confusions'. This model can be created only, Schön says, when there are close parallels between the practicum and real practice – when the coaching resembles the interpersonal practice to be learned. This is therefore a useful approach for mentors in ITE.

Schön also makes the important point that when coach and student do their jobs well they act as 'on-line researchers, each enquiring more or less consciously into his own and the other's changing understandings'. But it is clear that there can be no mastery of this. 'The behavioural world of the practicum is complex, variable and resistant to control' (see Schön 1987, p.298). The best that can be achieved is a willing co-operation in trying to grasp one's own and others' understandings. This understanding occurs when there is a public attempt to share and remains as tacit (inert) knowledge when there is no coach and no dialogue (see Schön 1987, pp.299–302).

Equipped with these perspectives we can now turn to Section 2 of this book and consider work with the student in the classroom.

Further reading

Schön, D. (1987) *Educating the reflective practitioner*. London: Jossey Bass. (Chapter 2, pp.22–40, is the most important follow-up reading for this chapter. It may need several readings. The first few pages are difficult, but the meat of the chapter is important.)

Other useful chapters or articles are as follows:

Carr, W. (1987) 'What is an educational practice?', *Journal of Philosophy of Education,* **21** (2), pp.163–75.

Fish, D. (1989) *Learning through practice in initial teacher training*. London: Kogan Page, pp.58–71.

McIntyre, D. (1993) 'Theory, theorizing and reflection in initial teacher education', in Calderhead, J. and Gates, P. (Eds) (1993) *Conceptualising reflection in teacher education*. London: Falmer Press, pp.39–52.

McIntyre, D. and Haggar, H. (1993) 'Teachers' expertise and models of mentoring', in McIntyre, D. *et al*. (Eds) (1993) *Mentoring: perspectives on school-based teacher education*. London: Kogan Page, pp.86–102.

Maynard, T. and Furlong, J. (1993) 'Learning to teach and models of mentoring', in McIntyre, D. *et al*. (Eds) (1993) *Mentoring: perspectives on school-based teacher education*. London: Kogan Page, pp.69–85.

Osterman, K. and Kottkamp, R. (1993) *Reflective practice for educators: improving schooling through professional development*. California: Corwin Press Inc. (See especially Chapters 2 and 8, pp.18–42 and 173–89.)

Russell, T. (1993a) 'Teachers' professional knowledge and the future of teacher education', in Gilroy, P. and Smith, M. (Eds) (1993) *International Analysis of Teacher Education/Journal of Teacher Education* (Double issue supplement), **19** (4/5), pp.205–15.

Russell, T. (1993b) 'Critical attributes of a reflective teacher: is agreement possible?', in Calderhead, J. and Gates, P. (Eds) (1993) *Conceptualising reflection in teacher development*. London: Falmer Press, pp.144–53.

Part 2

Classroom-focussed Mentoring:
A Quality Approach

CHAPTER 4

Quality Classroom Practice: Versions and Views of Good Practice

Introduction

It is generally held or implied in most government documents that good practice is a basic and essential concept in ITE and that questions about it need to be considered prior to (as well as continually during) working with a student in a school. It is therefore a concept that mentors need to consider carefully. But, in fact, good practice is both value-based and context specific. It is thus a rather more difficult notion than is implied. In the past it has often been the tacit and unexplored standard by which students have been judged. Now, since mentors are required to support the professional development and assess the achievements of students against competences, they cannot avoid making explicit, and discussing, the (imposed and arbitrary) standards by which they do so. (It should not, however, be assumed that the existence of competences will make assessment any more objective.) In addition to all this, mentors' own practice will be open to scrutiny by students who, in order to learn through it, will need, with the mentor's help, to discuss it in an appropriate language and to consider the processes involved in producing, developing and refining it. Alexander suggests that a minimum condition of partnership between schools and HE for ITE ought to be that the partners *each*:

> make explicit and argue their particular versions of good
> practice through to the point of consensus or its nearest
> approximation.
> (Alexander 1990, p.72)

This matters, he suggests, because it will help to establish a partnership of equals and will save difficulties later on. Such a move would not, however, necessarily mean that the partners would agree entirely between themselves, nor that they would endorse the government's approach to formulating and assessing good practice, even though they need to understand what each believes about it and although they must enact government requirements about competences.

Chapter 1 above established that all educational questions are value-based, and a little thought about the different skills needed with different classes will suggest that it is essentially context specific. Before tackling these matters in detail, we need to recognise that not one but a number of issues related to the meaning of good practice are at stake here, as the following set of questions attempts to reveal.

- What are the constituents of good practice?

- In what range of ways might it be analysed?

- Over how many aspects of professionalism should we seek good practice in beginning teachers?

- How might good practice be determined?

- How might we judge it?

- What would count as evidence?

- In what language might we usefully discuss good practice?

- What influential views already exist about good practice?

- How might we investigate practice?

- How do students see good practice?

- How might these views affect their observations and their practice?

- How might students be drawn to reconsider their views about good practice?

This chapter tackles these questions in three sections as follows: (i) a consideration of some concepts associated with good practice, some current influential versions of good practice, and some assumptions underlying both of these; (ii) a consideration of evidence for good practice and how practice might be investigated; (iii) students' ideas about good practice and how to help them refine these. Finally, some preliminary ideas about some principles of good practice in mentoring are offered as a lead into the following three chapters.

(i)

What constitutes good practice?

That professional activity which we value is that which we label good practice. Once again, the overall models of professional practice presented in Chapter 2 above serve to help us explore these issues. The following offers two polarised versions of these in order to enable mentors to explore their own views. As you consider the following paragraphs, you should bear in mind the possible distinction between your espoused theories and your theories-in-use.

Those who subscribe to the TR view of teaching accept a mastery of skills approach and therefore believe that good practice is about specifying and then mastering *the* necessary skills to a given, visible and measurable standard. Such skills they see as mainly classroom delivery skills. These are often considered to be subject or age-range (context) specific. This approach is considered to offer an objective means of assessing students' practice, though for some that objectivity is a chimera, being shot through with value-judgements at all points. Those who adopt the TR approach seek to establish *the* specific skills and their specific standards. To achieve this they either emphasise the development of competences (which have been listed by non-teachers) or they use the equally TR approach of employing empirical-analytic models established by research which seeks to develop 'a deductive system of ... scientific laws which [can] be used to predict and control teaching and learning' (see Diamond 1991, quoted in Bullough and Gitlin 1994, p.69). These versions of the TR approach beg all the questions about the criteria for deciding *the* skills, about how we can then master them, how many of them we must master to be a good practitioner and what (quantitatively and qualitatively) will count as evidence of our mastery. As Bullough and Gitlin also note, 'a good many battles have taken place ... particularly over determining what, precisely, beginning teachers ought to know and be able to do' (Bullough and Gitlin

1994, p.70). In this view, then, good practice is achieved as a result of someone outside the profession decreeing a standard, and by employing trainers to ensure its implementation (see Chapter 7 below). And the language in which good practice is discussed under this view is the confident language of the mastery of skills, but 'the beginning teacher's theories are ignored, or deemed illegitimate or irrelevant to learning to teach' (Bullough and Gitlin 1994, p.70).

Those who subscribe to the PA view eschew the notion that the essence of teaching is conveyed in pre-specifiable skills, do not believe that the same agenda of skills is necessary for everyone and reject the idea of mastery of professional practice. This does not mean, however, they pay no attention to skills but that these are discussed in terms of the principles upon which they are based and are attended to as they become significant in the practical setting. Those subscribing to this view consider teaching at the level of principle, seek to place teacher development within an educational framework, to develop a professional person rather than a skilled classroom deliverer. They seek to enable the prospective teacher to establish principled practice, the procedures of which will transcend specific contexts. Their aims involve attending to (their view of good practice includes) the development of professional insight from intuition, and the ability to exercise practical wisdom and professional judgement so that students know when and how to develop the skills they learn. They argue that we refine practice and our ideas about what is good practice by doing it, investigating it systematically and considering it in debate with others (clients, colleagues and writers). On this view, standards arise from professional improvement from within, and at the centre of this process is systematic reflection on practice which is also associated with seeking broader perspectives. As Broadhead says:

> good practice is much more than a string of seemingly successful classroom events. It is also the theoretical basis which each teacher brings to their practice. It is about understanding the learning process and about coming to terms with uncertainties and realities.
> (Broadhead 1990a, p.37)

And here we see, too, the tentative language of professional development in which good practice is discussed by those persuaded by this approach.

For some, then, striving for good practice is product-centred, that is, it is about trying to implement pre-decided skills. For others it is about processes and principles and involves continual seeking.

Various versions of good practice

The day-to-day working life of teachers is full of both formal and informal occasions on which professionals and non-professionals make judgements about teachers and teaching, for example: OFSTED formal inspections; interview panels; appraisal interviews; teaching practice; research reports; parents' evenings; staffroom talk; parent informal talk; pupil grapevines. Some of these judgements are often made on the basis of very little – *if any* – empirical evidence. Only the most formal of these occasions ever state the criteria against which such judgements are made, and then those criteria are not always central to the final decisions. It is thus a major question as to whether specific criteria or rules and procedures set down external to the individual context are ever of any great value in considering good practice and assessing teaching or whether recourse to considering the teacher's operating principles is more useful.

The TR view of teaching, as we have seen, embraces inspection and control occasions. For its adherents, objectively stated examples of good practice are important. Yet, even as they have tried to express what they believe about good practice, the DES and HMI have revealed the very problems endemic to this process. Their early attempts to raise standards in the profession by reference to models of good practice have been analysed in detail by Broadhead and shown to fall very short of providing useful detail about good practice for thoughtful teachers. She looked at a number of significant publications, from DES/HMI in the late 1970s to the early 1980s, which addressed issues related to the identification of 'good teaching' (*Primary education in England* (1978); *Better schools* (1982); *Education observed 3: good teachers* (1982); *Teaching quality* (1983); *The new teacher in school* (1983)). She reported that these papers reveal a 'lack of classroom exemplars' (Broadhead 1987, p.68), that no reference is made to a framework of self-improvement, that the models focus only on the end product of an ideal teacher, that they fail to address the detailed complexity of the primary classroom, and that they suggest strongly that by acquiring certain behaviours teachers will improve their classroom efficiency (Broadhead 1987, pp.68–9). Thus, they are stereotypical and ignore the complexity of real classrooms.

However, there is also a problem with the opposite approach.

Government documents which lay down case studies of individual good teachers and then deduce from these some rules of good practice to be applied generally, offer advice that is distorted by being generalised from the particular and which may be inappropriate if applied to other situations. A prime example of this kind of document is OFSTED's *Well-managed classes in primary schools: case studies of six teachers* which was published in 1993. This small study, conducted in 1991, is addressed to teachers who, whilst 'not required to teach or organise their classes in prescribed ways' are nevertheless 'expected to keep their teaching and organisation under review to see how far they are contributing to the implementation of the National Curriculum, and, where necessary, to make modifications' (OFSTED 1993d, p.1). This document contains cases of teachers whom, it says, are effective but not exceptional. The report emphasises that there is no one 'best buy', but that what is important is a 'variety of modes of organisation and teaching, chosen with the criterion fitness for purpose in mind and flexibly deployed' (OFSTED 1993d, p.2).

However, the criterion 'fitness for purpose' is purely about the instrumental aspects of teaching – that is, the means by which the National Curriculum can be efficiently delivered. It takes no account of ends or of the moral aspects of the means. Interestingly, too, the case studies are followed by a four-page summary of the characteristics of a well-managed class, with on average nine points each under the headings: 'Planning for Teaching'; 'Classroom Context'; 'Assessment Diagnosis and Task-setting'; 'Organisational Strategies'; 'Teaching Techniques'. Although there is a disclaimer at the end, making the point that the list is 'not exhaustive' and that 'practice is inevitably richer and more complex than written accounts can capture' (OFSTED 1993d, p.32), there is clearly a thrust towards being able to specify the rules of behaviour that the writers believe make up good practice. Thus, deriving rules and procedures for good practice (whether starting from specific cases or general surveys) is fraught with problems. Working at the level of principle is perhaps more useful, since it offers ways of deciding how to operate in context but does not try to tell professionals what to do and when.

In contrast with government agents' attempts to solve the problem of modelling good practice, Brown and McIntyre have usefully uncovered some themes common to a range of good teachers *and* the language in which the teachers themselves characterise them. These could be used, not to train students to reproduce them, but as an aid to discussing good practice. The teachers in this research described and evaluated what they were doing in the following terms:

- how they maintain the interest and enthusiasm of their pupils
- how they diffuse actual or potential discipline problems
- how their planning interacts with their management of classes and of lessons
- their approaches to taking account of the characteristics of individual pupils
- the ways in which they deal with pupils' errors
- their attempts to build up confidence and trust with pupils
- how they manage their introductions to the lessons
- how they provide help for pupils
- how they manage question and answer sessions.
  (Brown and McIntyre 1993, p.39)

This research offers vignettes, and detailed individual examples, which are useful in working with student teachers. Brown and McIntyre are also very careful how they generalise from these, making the points that they do so 'by seeking common concepts across teachers in the ways in which they evaluate and talk about their teaching' and that their generalisations are 'naturalistic' and 'form the basis of hypotheses to be carried on from one case to the next', rather than 'probabilistic' arising from the application of statistics to data, which would aim to generalise across the whole population of teachers (Brown and McIntyre 1993, p.50). However, in spite of this, and of its possible uses to aid reflection on practice, this work is still influenced by a TR view of professionalism, which needs to be borne in mind as it is used.

For those who espouse the PA approach, the judgements which are most valuable and which often most powerfully influence and refine practice are those made by teachers about themselves in the light of investigating their actions, and enlightening their findings by reference to the work of others (colleagues/writers). From such investigations, principles of procedure can be built. To this end, a vital set of processes in ITE provide the means to investigate personal practice. By using such processes, which include entering into dialogue with the situation and bringing to it critical perspectives from the work of others, the professional artist is educated. And this process does not have to wait until certain basic skills are 'under the student's belt', but can be employed from the very beginning as a *modus operandi* which is built into the very foundation of professional practice. For this reason, the following section looks in some detail at investigating practice. First, however, mentors may need to review something of their own practice and their views about good practice.

Good practice in the mentor's classroom

Most courses in ITE begin with students observing the mentor. Such observation, if it is to be of any use, will need to be discussed with the student (see Chapter 5 below). There is thus no doubt that the mentor will need to be well aware of the strengths and problems of his/her own practice and be able to discuss this with students. As Alexander points out, good practice is a notion which is also about 'a classroom's potential for the *student's* as well as the child's learning' (Alexander 1990, p.67). In fact McIntyre makes the point that since school classrooms have become the dominant contexts for student teachers' learning, this shift towards more school-based ITE creates the opportunity, but only the *opportunity*, to make classrooms more helpful learning environments for both students and pupils (McIntyre 1994, p.81). As he also points out, great benefits to students will not occur, however, unless mentors see themselves and their classrooms in a new light and work towards providing for students' *learning* (rather than just for their teaching practice) during placement (see McIntyre 1994).

Providing a learning environment involves teachers being able to articulate clearly what is involved in their teaching. But, for some very good reasons, this has proved difficult. As Brown and McIntyre point out, teachers see what happens in their lessons as 'so ordinary and so obvious as not to merit any comment'. They also suggest that teachers often have difficulty in: 'explicitly describing their routine patterns of activity, and particularly in formulating the ways in which they make their decisions ...' And they make the point that to offer an account of 'what one does spontaneously, even unconsciously, every day is a most demanding task which the individual teacher is rarely called upon to do' (Brown and McIntyre 1993, pp.13–14). Yet to be able to discuss a lesson observed and to be able to pinpoint those elements of good practice in it and its underlying principles of procedure will be basic to working with students, since students need to be taught what it is they are looking at. Mentors clearly will need to build up experience of this. To that end the following task is offered.

TASK 4.1: POINTS FOR ACTION AND DISCUSSION

Use one side of one piece of A4 for the first three questions.

1. Write down your key views on what is good practice in teaching. Take a bit of time on this – don't just dash down the first two things you think of. Imagine that you might be addressing a colleague in preparation for having a student.

2. Write down your essential views about pupils' learning. (Audience as above.)

3. Write down (briefly!) your *school's* essential views about teaching and learning and assessment. (What is your *evidence* for them?)

4. *On a clean sheet of A4 paper using one side only* describe in detail, as to a colleague from another institution or a student who had watched one of your lessons, but might have missed the detail, a *small* piece of your own practice (perhaps part of a lesson – certainly not more than one whole lesson) of which you have recently been particularly proud. Don't get too hung up on explaining the contextual details – say the minimum necessary for an outsider to grasp your main issues. Say more about the meat of the good practice. Use points. Tell the story of the lesson or part of it.

5. *On a separate A4 sheet, using one side only*, say as exactly as possible *why* it was good practice. What was good about it? Explain as to a student the key aspects of its good practice.

6. Share your written responses to Question 4 with a colleague with whom you don't usually work.

7. Ask the colleague to deduce and jot down what seem to be your views on teaching and learning that underlie your description of practice.

8. Compare what your colleague wrote with your own comments in answer to Question 5. Any points additional to your own may show theories/values/beliefs that you were not aware of.

Any key differences between your answers to Questions 1 and 2 and to Question 5 may indicate a tension between your beliefs about good practice and your actual practice (your espoused theories and your theories-in-use).

Equally, it is important to recognise that there is an element of subjectivity in all of this, and that underlying the whole exercise are views about good practice which need to be further examined.

Looking at oneself, one's practice and one's underlying views of good practice (beliefs/assumptions/theories) in this way can be decidedly uncomfortable. As Jennifer Nias points out, it involves seeing oneself anew, and this brings with it additional anxiety and vulnerability (Nias 1987, p.13). As Broadhead says, perception is not just seeing, but involves interpretation, the ability to distinguish between crucial and less important issues in teaching and learning and to discern meaning from what is seen (Broadhead 1990b, p.126). Speaking of using video to capture and investigate one's practice, she points out the 'feelings of dis-equilibrium that viewers of self may experience ... as they attempt to reconcile what they see of themselves and the impact of their actions on the classroom, [compared] with an inner conviction of what they believe themselves to be doing and the impact they believe it is having' (Broadhead 1990b, p.127). She also lists, as follows, seven questions that viewers ask of their work when it is first video-ed, and which teachers preparing to work as mentors, and therefore to open their practice to critical scrutiny of others, might also find a useful starting point.

- Do I look like the teacher I think I am?
- Do I look like the person I think I am?
- Am I behaving in ways in which I think I behave?
- Will others see me as I see myself?
- Do I want to modify the image I have of myself?
- How easy will that be?
- What are the implications for my practice?
  (Broadhead 1990b, p.134)

However, we should note carefully that observable evidence is also liable to misinterpretation since what is visible is often ambiguous and is rarely the whole story. It is usually necessary therefore to consider a range of perspectives on the issue in question.

TASK 4.2: POINTS FOR ACTION

1. Set up a video camera in part of a lesson which you would like to investigate or ask a colleague to video you (about twenty minutes is all you will need).

Or/and, on another occasion, set up a tape recorder while you work with a group of pupils.

2. Review the tape afterwards in private and with plenty of time to think about it.

3. Ask yourself the questions immediately above.

4. Recapture if possible what you were thinking as you worked (your reflections-in-action).

5. Ask pupils (and any other adult present) what they thought was happening in that part of the lesson. (These are ways of gaining other perspectives on, and other interpretations of, events.)

And so we begin to see the need to investigate our practice more systematically. Mentors will need to discuss with students this approach to learning practice − and even to offer themselves as an example of doing so. The following section offers some perspectives on this.

(ii)

Learning good practice: a contribution from research

It is clear, then, from the above that there are a number of ways in which research knowledge about teaching and learning can be harnessed by professionals in pursuit of improving their practice or of achieving good practice. For example, they can use research conducted by others for a variety of purposes, or they can conduct their own investigations. Before the practitioner is able to take advantage of any of these, however, she/he needs to understand how different approaches to research operate. The following two subsections attempt to explain the broad differences between the main research approaches and to offer some ways in which teachers can investigate their own practice.

Extending understanding or proving the point?

There is, even amongst professionals, a tendency to equate research with the gathering of large quantities of data in pursuit of proving hypotheses. But this is only one approach to research, which lies within the scientific domain, world-view or 'paradigm' of research, and whose bases are found in scientific methods. It operates on a large scale and views its findings as hard knowledge which professional practitioners should find their own ways of implementing. Its language is the language of proof and evidence. It seeks to provide a foundation in knowing. That is, it seeks truth. It is reductionist in that the scale of its operations requires a recourse to reducing ideas to numbers or models. It claims to be objective. It does not always draw attention to the fact that its findings are themselves only *theories*. For practitioners the advantages of outside researchers (people whose profession is researching rather than teaching) are that they can offer a fresh view of practice. It, however, always simplifies the true complexities of school and classroom life and, in its processes, results and recommendations, does not always take full account of the real requirements of a professional. The TR view tends to look to this sort of research to help in the improvement of practice. But, in fact, as Russell reminds us:

> it is professional delusion to assume that our practices proceed from a set of deliberate, tested premises about how pupils or teachers learn, no matter how much 'theory' one has studied.
> (Russell 1993a, p.207)

An alternative approach is that of the humanistic or interpretative paradigm of research. Its bases are found in the social sciences and many of its methods are derived from the arts. It operates on a small scale and seeks to understand the individual case rather than to prove knowledge on a large scale. That is, it seeks wisdom. This broad approach provides a means for the individual practitioner to find out about and to understand his/her practice better.

Taking an investigative stance to practice

To be a reflective practitioner is to be committed to reflection on and investigation of one's practice in order to refine and improve it continuously. This approach is seen by many as an essential part of quality teaching. This means that teaching and research are seen as closely interrelated. Indeed, reflection may be both a means of investigating practice and the stimulus for further investigation.

The *audience* for this may be personal. It may be one's colleagues (shared through INSET; or in professional appraisal). It may be the wider reading world. By sharing ideas and the fruits of investigation we are all the gainers in improved understanding and perhaps refined practice. Importantly, for the mentor, the audience may (some might argue 'should') be one's student teacher.

There seems, then, to be little doubt that investigating one's practice is a natural part of learning to teach – or at least – of being a professional, reflective teacher. Investigation of one's practice can be on a very small and personal scale and need not take up much time in addition to one's professional engagements. One can take a look at a part of one lesson and can enlighten, refine and improve practice and re-enliven work that might otherwise become routine. As Rudduck says:

> After a while, teachers see what they expect to see and constantly reconstruct the classroom in its own image. Reflective research is a way of helping teachers to sharpen their perceptions of the everyday realities of their work; it helps them to identify worthwhile problems to work on, and through their enquiry to extend their own understanding, insight and command of the situations in which they work.

This, she argues, enables teachers to see the 'contradictions of purpose and value' in their work, and to monitor whether their strategies achieve their intended purpose. She adds, significantly for mentors:

> the likelihood of teachers opting to learn from the thoughtful and critical study of their own practice is greater if such activity has been legitimized during initial training.
> (Rudduck 1992, p.164)

The more difficult question is how best to do this. Some would argue that reflective research is enough; some say that critical action research is an important means to this; some prefer the development of small-scale practitioner-focussed case study.

Reflective research involves investigating one's immediate working arena with a view to improving it as a result of reflecting upon it. Rudduck argues that it:

> is a way of building personal excitement, confidence and insight – and these are important foundations for career-long personal and professional development.
> (Rudduck 1992, p.165)

By contrast to this, action research is less exclusively classroom-focussed and sees reflection as less significant than action, emphasising the changes to be made to future practice rather more than the understanding of present practice.

However, in all research, the aims and the focus of the investigation are most significant, and they can sometimes cause the research approach to seem unnecessarily limited. Just as there can be a simplistic and inward-looking version of reflective research which aims only at inert reflection, so, too, there can exist a simplistic version of action research which rushes precipitately into action aimed at change, where there is little overt recognition of some of the more problematic aspects of education and no way of ensuring that the moral and ethical aspects of a teacher's work are attended to. This is why Van Manen (1990) warns against action research (though the pitfalls can be avoided if the investigator has wider horizons and takes account of wider views). Johnston (1994) indicates the kinds of barriers that she believes make this process less than natural to busy teachers.

Golby argues that 'case study, properly conceived, is uniquely appropriate as a form of educational research for practitioners to conduct. It has the potential to relate theory and practice, advancing professional knowledge by academic means' (Golby 1993c, pp.3−4). He argues that case study is 'not the name of a method but more a signal that a concrete instance is to be investigated' and that the enquirer will use any tools which are appropriate to the question and the situation (see Golby 1989, p.168). Case study allows for the study of 'particular incidents and events, and the selective collection of information on biography, personality, intentions and values, [which] allows the case study worker to capture and portray those elements of a situation that give it meaning' (Walker 1986, p.189). Case study is a systematising of experience which has the quality of undeniability. Such studies are 'intensive investigations of single cases which both serve to identify and describe basic phenomena, as well as provide the basis for subsequent theory development' (Kenny and Grotelleuschen 1984, p.37). Case study can be merely descriptive, can be analytical or can be deliberative. As Golby explains, generalisation from such study can be made only when the *particular* rather than the *unique* nature of the study is identified − that is, when it is clear what the particular case is a case of. The unique, by its very nature, is unable to be thus classified, and it therefore becomes impossible to discuss it in general terms (see especially Golby 1993c, pp.6−9; and also Fish and Purr 1991, p.23). Case study can thus, very usefully, provide the data for reflection on detailed practice and its wider implications.

There is evidence, then, that it is possible for teachers to take on a research/inquiry dimension in their teaching, via reflective research, critical action research or case study particularly, and that the activities of reflection and of producing narratives of classrooms and schools provide a language in which to discuss teaching and learning to teach. Readers are directed to the extensive literature on enquiry methods in qualitative research if they wish to pursue these matters further.

We must remember, though, that student teachers bring their own knowledge to learning practice. Included in that knowledge are their own views about good practice, which must be attended to.

(iii)

Students' views of good practice

Since all students have had at least thirteen years' experience of schooling before joining HE, they tend to regard themselves as experts on how to teach, not recognising that there are aspects of teaching that they have not seen. Their experiences of the smooth and fluent performances of their own teachers have obscured the underlying work. This is sometimes why teachers' extensive planning comes as a shock. It is why the moral dimensions of teaching are new ground. It is why they think that learning to teach is a matter of common sense and copying a good teacher or mastering a few skills. It is why students sometimes say or write ill-informed critiques of professional lessons they have observed. In short, one of the key tasks in the early part of a course is to work on students' views of good practice. Kyriacou reviews research on student teachers' knowledge and understanding, some of which shows vividly how their ideas have to be worked on at the abstract level and not just at the level of practice, in order that their images of teaching develop and become 'better informed, realistic, relevant and usable' (Kyriacou 1993, p.80).

How tutors work on these

Tutors have traditionally worked with and on those views of good practice that students bring with them to an ITE course, especially at the start of the course and before they first go into school. Elizabeth Dunne describes offering vignettes of teachers' practices to students as a way of eliciting their beliefs about teaching (Dunne 1993). But it is Bullough and Gitlin (1994), who offer a clear explanation of the important thrust of work with students in this area. They say that:

> our conceptions of ourselves as teachers are grounded biographically. If teacher education is to make a difference, it must start with biography and find ways to identify, clarify, articulate and critique the assumptions – the personal theories – about teaching, learning, students, and education embedded within it.
> (Bullough and Gitlin 1994, p.76)

There is a need for students to be able to work on these ideas at a distance from schools. The processes are quite sophisticated, and teachers are rarely aware of what tutors do in this respect. In most ITE courses this involves a number of moves. Tutors first work with students on their own autobiographical descriptions of their schooling, on video examples of practice or on shared observations of class teaching and on students' own descriptions of their own early attempts at teaching. They draw students to articulate their critiques of teaching experienced, observed and carried out.

Attention is given to the texture of the language used by the students, and to the underlying beliefs and assumptions. By this means the students' tacit views about good practice are made explicit. These views are then open to public discussion and thus to reconsideration and to challenge. The tutor's task here is to ensure that students become aware of alternatives and that students also begin to recognise that uncertainty and the admission of ignorance are the means to further learning. This process can, of course, be painful, but without it little progress can be made in learning through practice.

Time is needed for this to have effect and for revisiting the crudity of the emerging notions. Direct challenge is not always helpful at this point. Neither is offence at student critique. Discussion needs to be managed by someone who is unchallenged personally by students' comments and who enables the students to work through their views and to see for themselves the need to modify them. This, then, is yet another dimension of enabling students to learn through practice. But it requires distance in space and time from the practice setting. Tutors have come to see it as enabling students to find their own voices (see Fish 1995). Some are now wondering how mentors on school-centred ITT courses will fare in taking over this aspect of work, since, when students observe teachers in the earliest stages of their course, their very observations are strongly affected by their own notions of good practice, and they often comment on lessons observed in strong and inappropriate language. Teachers who do not understand this can be hurt and affronted by what are often quite guileless comments. This is why being observed is at least as demanding as observing a student. But that is to move on to matters dealt with in Chapter 5 below. First it remains to consider what we can now say about good practice in mentoring itself.

(iv)

Good practice in mentoring

Clearly students consider teachers to have a wide range of knowledge, which will help them learn to teach, but there is often a lack of understanding on the part of both students and teachers about how students might gain access to it. This is because we are now so conditioned by the 'delivery' metaphor to think of teaching as 'giving to others' that the key notion of facilitating learners to learn for themselves easily slips out of our sight. If, however, the processes of learning through practice as described in Chapter 3 above have anything to teach us about good mentoring practices, it is, arguably, that facilitating learning is a vital approach for the mentor. Readers are now invited to consider critically the following suggested principles of good mentoring practice.

- A mentor is a facilitator who empowers practitioners and draws them to learn for themselves by reflecting on practice.

- Reflection and learning processes are more important than 'coverage', so experiential learning is an important vehicle.

- The mentor is *not* an expert 'knower'. Student learners already have much knowledge and need to be jolted out of being authority dependent. They need to recognise what they know and can do and which parts of their work need developing or refining.

- Mentors need the skills, abilities and capacity to enable learners to learn through practice and to (re)construct their own knowledge for themselves and each other by deliberating together. Mentors need to be able to set the atmosphere for this and to establish norms and modes of operation that foster that sort of learning.

- Mentoring is about helping learners to question the taken-for-granted and to see things anew – even to go on wondering/worrying at issues long after the session.

- Disagreements (impersonal ones) are a major means of learning. Passion can get in the way. Mentors need to keep the balance between objectivity and passion.

- Evidence and reasoning are vital in enabling students to recognise their values/beliefs, reconsider them, 'know them for the first time' and *then* decide what to do about them. Mentors need to discipline the debate and order the processes.

- A mentor's role is to defend everyone's right to be heard, but to encourage the hearers to think/challenge/question and offer their *considered* view.

- It is very important for the mentor to create a climate in which it is safe for students to learn and to bare their real views, ideas, beliefs, and also their errors and problems (which are the learning points of practice).

- Mentors need to establish the fact that ambiguity and uncertainty are the important norms. Students need to see that 'knowing for sure' is suspect in learning professional practice.

- The agenda needs to include inquiry into everything. A mentor's role is to be an example of an inquiring and reflective practitioner – to be prepared to be made the *subject* of inquiry by the learning group!

- A mentor's role is to support while also challenging. Challenge should not be destructive. A mentor therefore needs to know well and be comfortable with both these issues and these processes.

- A mentor's practice should show that learning makes one less certain, not more. Learning is about saying '*I think* X', not '*You* should think X' or 'I *know* X'. Mentoring is not about telling the student.

- Mentors need to be able to be challenged and look deeply at their own practice and have disagreements about it without getting personally/emotionally thrown. Looking in depth at even a small piece of one's practice can be very alarming.

- Mentors need to be able to help students to respond positively to challenge, to support them in this and to know how to handle the issues about evidence.

- A mentor's assessment of a student should show evidence of the important kinds of learning described/implied above, as well as of classroom skills.

Mentors will wish to consider the value-base of these statements and how far they are in agreement with them.

Quality mentoring, then, is mentoring practice which is based upon an understanding of educational principles. Having considered these matters it is now time to turn to the detail of working with students.

Further reading

Alexander, R. (1990) 'Partnership in initial teacher education: confronting the issues', in Booth, M. *et al.* (Eds) (1990) *Partnership in initial teacher training.* London: Cassell, pp.59–73.

Anning, A. *et al.* (1990) *Using video-recording for teacher professional development.* Leeds: University of Leeds, School of Education.

Bell, J. *et al.* (1984) *Conducting small-scale investigations in educational management.* London: Harper & Row.

Brown, S. and McIntyre, D. (1993) *Making sense of teaching.* Buckingham: Open University Press.

Bullough, R. and Gitlin, A. (1994) 'Challenging teacher education as training: four propositions', *Journal of Education for Teaching*, **20** (1), pp.67–81.

Hopkins, D. (1985) *A teacher's guide to classroom research.* Milton Keynes: Open University Press.

Kyriacou, C. (1993) 'Research on the development of expertise in classroom teaching during initial teacher training and the first year of teaching', *Educational Review*, **45** (1), pp.78–88.

Nias, J. (1987) *Seeing anew: teachers' theories of action.* Geelong: Deakin University.

CHAPTER 5

Observing Students and Being Observed

Introduction

In an ITE programme observation can enable the student to watch the mentor, the mentor to observe the student or both of them to observe a third party. The use of video extends this to enable the student to watch him/herself. Observation is a central tool of learning as well as of assessment in ITE. But, if it is used inappropriately, without a clear purpose, and in ignorance of its nature and its potential as an approach to finding out about teaching, it can provide a thoroughly unhelpful experience not only for students but also for mentors. It can also produce highly distorted evidence about the achievements of teaching.

Observation is a research technique, and there are a number of investigative tools associated with it, each of which is a specialist implement. It is the nature of observation to concentrate only on the known and visible aspects of a performance. Some of the most important aspects of children's learning and teachers' fostering of this are not easily seen. The smooth surface of good practice often renders them invisible. Equally, the surface failure of a particular teaching performance does not necessarily mean that the teacher is a failure. Thus, when, how and why to employ observation as an approach to enabling students to learn to teach, and what it can tell one about teaching, all need to be carefully considered by the mentor.

This chapter seeks to enable mentors to think about some useful principles of observation in ITE and suggests some tasks which will enable them to investigate these principles further. It considers the nature of observation and focusses on the mentor operating as observer of the student and on the student observing the mentor. In either case the overall intention of most observation is to enable meaning to emerge from the experience, just as was attempted in Chapter 3 above. It should be noted that the post-lesson discussion (known as follow-up or debriefing) is a vital aspect of this whole process. But in order to treat this in detail it has been reserved until the following chapter.

(i)

The nature and uses of observation in ITE

There is nothing to be gained, by the teacher or student, from a mentor dropping into a lesson for an off-the-cuff observation which has neither been prepared beforehand nor will be followed up afterwards. This section attempts to delineate some of the likely issues about observation which mentors will need to consider in planning an observation.

The roles of observation in an ITE programme

Observation of teachers is used for a range of reasons in the teaching profession. It is a pity that, because it is used in teaching practice assessment, appraisal, and even in the case of failing teachers, many of the occasions on which classroom observation occurs are associated with making momentous judgements about teachers' careers. By contrast, observation of teaching is perhaps at its most useful when used as an approach to help teachers and students to *learn* about and to refine their teaching.

To be useful in this way on an ITE course, the role of observation in the student's overall programme needs to be known and understood by both parties. This can best be achieved if thought has been given to the range of activities that can help a student teach (that is, can lead them to the ultimate unsheltered activity of teaching a whole class alone). Cameron-Jones offers a broad framework for drawing a student to learn to teach, which may help to set observation in context. She discusses what she calls 'thought-oriented methods' where practical matters are aimed at provoking thinking (like explaining, exploring or discussing the traditions of the profession; using a teacher as a model to consider aspects of teaching; discussing case studies; filling in or altering scripts of incidents; and posing dilemmas). These she distinguishes from methods that involve the student in teaching. Here she points to methods that engage the student gradually in the practice of teaching, like: isolating a particular skill, strategy or style of teaching; peer teaching; devising small-scale activities to use with groups of children; and setting up paired teaching (see Cameron-Jones 1991).

Most ITE programmes utilise all of these techniques. Some of them, until now, have traditionally taken place in college and have not been visible to school teachers. Many of the things that students need to learn cannot be pinpointed by observation alone. It is often necessary to combine observation with interviews or discussion in order to reach the invisible aspects of teaching. Thus, observation is *one* of the methods of finding out about teaching.

The importance of purpose in observation

Following Cameron-Jones' classification of different ways of learning about teaching, we can see that observation can contribute to a range of purposes, provoking students to think or prompting them to act, as well as being a means of collecting evidence for judgements to be made. Thus, whenever it is used, its purposes must be carefully defined. As Haggar, Burn and McIntyre point out, 'Unfocused observation, without a clear purpose is generally demoralising and counter-productive' (Haggar, Burn and McIntyre 1993, p.26).

Once the overall purpose is clear, then the focus for the observation, the specific tools for observing, the methods of recording and the ways in which this whole process might be learnt from can all be decided. But though very useful, these tools are also highly dangerous, and they need to be employed in the fullest possible knowledge of their strengths and weaknesses. The following section looks at the detail of this.

Techniques for observing and their strengths and weaknesses

Most books on investigating professional practice (for example: Burgess 1985; Hopkins 1985; and Walker 1985) offer details about classroom observation. The following can offer only an overview. The techniques and strategies used will need to be appropriate to the focus of the observation. This will depend upon what they can and cannot achieve. What is observed can be narrow or wide in focus. How it is observed will depend upon the overall purpose of the observation. The following represent the major techniques.

Some of them emphasise the quantitative approach and seek to reduce what is observed to numbers; some emphasise the qualitative approach which attempts to recognise and preserve the rich complexity of human situations. Proponents of the quantitative approach claim objectivity for it, but in fact this is spurious since subjective judgements are being made at all points in classifying information.

It is possible to take an unstructured approach to observation. That is, it is possible to observe in a naturalistic way without predetermined categories (to watch with an open mind and see what happens). While enabling the observer to see what happens, it can also result in failure to notice some quantitative details. It is often used as a first step to narrowing down an observation focus or a research question and can be a useful means of learning about the student as a teacher generally.

It is possible to observe using schedules and checklists. In this case, the categories need to be clear. Categories help observers to see some things but blind them to those they have not predetermined. It is regarded as objective, though, as we have seen above this is not the case. Too many categories can make an observation schedule impossible to use in practice.

It is possible to use a ratings approach. Here a coded scale is set up, and the observer rates the occurrence of a particular behaviour, using graphic, numerical or categorical rating scales. The emphasis here is on the number of times a category occurs. Like the checklist approach, it is regarded as objective, though of course judgements are being made each time something is categorised. It is also blinkered and can blind the observer to other issues.

Another dimension that should be considered in observation is the role of the observer in the practice being observed. In participant observation the observer is a normal member of the group, joins in wholeheartedly with the activities, events, behaviours and culture of the group and may not even be known as an observer/investigator or mentor by the group. The investigator here gains meaning through personal participation. It is not observation alone that informs his/her understanding of the action. This approach offers a better grasp of the complexities of the situation. But it is clearly very subjective, and the observer can affect the very practice she/he is observing.

In non-participant observation the investigator is unobtrusive, does not engage in the work of the group as a group member, but remains aloof and distanced from the action. She/he certainly does not feign membership of the group. The observation here is concerned only with participants' behaviours. The focus is on valid recording of behaviours using an unobtrusive strategy of data collection, so as not to interfere with the natural sequence of events. Care is taken not to disturb the ethos and culture of the setting. Yet only the visible is recorded.

It is quite possible to use (in a thoughtful and informed way) a mixture of these versions. It is also important to think about how they might be supplemented by procedures that will provide complementary data, like interviews, tape-recording of a group, video camera, stop-frame photography, documentary analysis. Being systematic is important. But the observer always needs to have thought through the strengths, weaknesses and specific possibilities of the approach being used. Account also needs to be taken of the kind of data that will be generated by the chosen techniques, how this will be captured (recorded) and how it will be used in the post-lesson discussion.

Some problematic issues

While much of the above seems to suggest that issues in observation are cut and dried, it is the case that many aspects of it are problematic. For example, there is no such thing as purely objective, factual, observation. All seeing is selective, and all reporting of what is seen is interpretative. Thus, in all observations the 'facts' are coloured by at least two filters. And this is true whatever method of observing and recording is adopted. For example, even an observer who seeks and notes down specific instances of a particular behaviour on a checklist (which might seem to be a matter of recording pure facts) is actually interpreting behaviours before deciding which can be counted as specific behaviours to be recorded. And when she/he categorises them fairly crudely on paper she/he will also be ignoring other aspects of the classroom which might have cast a different light on what is being observed. Equally, observers who record in words rather than figures will inevitably indicate some kind of judgement of the situation observed in their choice of expression. Further, with such a human and variable activity as teaching, there are likely to be many possible interpretations of most events and the best that an observer can do is to seek several differing perspectives on the event and a range of possible interpretations of it. The following task will enable readers to investigate this for themselves.

TASK 5.1: POINTS FOR INVESTIGATION

1.   Video or tape-record about fifteen minutes of the beginning of a lesson, either yours or a colleague's.

2.   Invite several colleagues (or students), without any discussion of the lesson beforehand, to watch the video through *once only* and as they watch (and for a few minutes afterwards) to write a clear, simple description of exactly what was happening in the first ten to fifteen minutes. The teacher of the lesson should also do this.

3.   Compare what each observer has written. (Exclude the teacher of the lesson from this exercise.)

4.   Look in detail at the differences between narratives and try to decide why people have written different things — go back to replay the video if you wish to at this point.

5.   Compare what observers thought with what the teacher thought was happening.

6.   If you have the chance, find out how the pupils saw that first fifteen minutes.

7.   What have you learnt about observation?

What we can now say, then, is that the observer deals not in simple facts but in a version or versions of these. Some useful distinctions are those between analysis (the atomising of what is seen into its component parts), interpretation (a version or versions of what has been seen from a particular point or points of view) and an appreciation of what has been observed (an artistic critique of what has been seen which emphasises recognition of its successes and failures).

One further matter relates to these issues. We have already seen, in Chapter 3, that unearthing the theories-in-use in teaching is a useful means of understanding how a student (or teacher) thinks and of seeing what informs their professional judgements. It is also important for the observer to be aware of the theories-in-use (both those about teaching and those about observation) that direct his/her observation, in order to take account of these and to try to keep some balanced judgement about the lesson seen. This is especially important if, for example, the observer is watching activities that run contrary to his/her own preferred way of teaching.

TASK 5.2: POINTS FOR INVESTIGATION

Return to the previous task and ask yourself:

- What theories-in-use directed the teacher's activities?
- What theories-in-use shaped the observations and interpretations offered?
- What does this reveal about observation?

Finally, it is also important to be aware of the complex nature of evidence − both what counts as evidence during observation and what it might be evidence of. In the TR view of professionalism, the evidence sought by an observer is that recorded behaviour which will prove correct the judgements that have been made. There are problems here, however, in that (because of the lack of objectivity in observation) it is difficult to know what some behaviours are evidence of, and it is difficult to be sure how often a behaviour should occur before it can be regarded as definitely evidence of a particular judgement. The PA approach renders this less of a problem since the observer here will seek out critical incidents in a lesson observed and then consult the views and understanding of the observed in order to disentangle what rationale actually informed the action. Here, the recorded observations offer the basis for discussion rather than providing evidence in terms of proof, and the reasons for the observer's judgements then spring from the ideas as well as the actions of the teacher observed.

Equipped with these general principles and issues, now let us turn to the two main aspects of observation: the mentor being observed and then the mentor observing.

(ii)

The mentor being observed

The beginning of an ITE course usually includes opportunities for the student to think about his/her own teaching by means of observing a variety of teachers at work. Some of those observed will be staff with whom the student rarely works. All, however, have responsibilities for working as mentors and making the observation an educational experience. This is why such observations need to focus not on how to reproduce the teaching observed, but on using what is seen as a means for the student to consider his/her own preferred approaches. But in order to do so, mentors need to be aware that students can find observation unhelpful as a result of the following conditions:

- The experienced teacher being watched is so fluent that it looks easy, and no one helps them to see underneath the performance to the expertise. (The teacher's skill here is often in expert information-processing and speedy decision-making that he/she is hardly aware of him/herself!)

- Students see only what they understand already. They certainly don't understand the complexity of teaching. The teacher needs to be articulate about its complexity and to be able to talk with the student about the issues related to 'good practice'.

- Students have already spent thousands of hours in the classroom – as pupils. They come at first with their pupil perspectives and find it difficult to see situations as teachers do.

- Students often have strong preconceptions about what sort of teachers they want to be. They are quick to judge those teachers whom they think are falling short of these preconceptions and therefore to think that they have little to learn from them.

- Students are generally keen to prove themselves as teachers. They are eager to get on with teaching and to learn from their own practice rather than learning from others.
(With acknowledgement to Haggar, Burn and McIntyre 1993)

Clarifying the purpose of observation

We have already said that having a clear purpose for observation is vital to its usefulness. There is a range of purposes for involving students in observing experienced teachers. Students need to understand in advance of observing: the teacher's intentions for the lesson; the context of the observation; and the learning intentions of the observation itself for the student-observer. The student will only really learn from the observation where the mentor follows it up with the student, both in an open way and by ensuring that pre-determined issues have been discussed. Thus, mentors need to work with the student in discussing the purpose, deciding the focus of the observation, understanding the context, showing the student how to observe and record and in helping the student to use and learn from interpretation, analysis and appreciation of what happened. The following reasons (shown in bold print) for observing experienced teachers have been listed by Haggar, Burn and McIntyre (1993). The explanations below each item offer a summary of their ideas.

1. It helps students shift from pupil-perspectives to teacher-perspectives at the beginning of a course.
In order to recognise how much they have to learn, students need to see difficult classes, and to hear teachers *analysing* their own less-than-perfect practice and considering alternative methods. They need to consider questions like: What would I do now? What are the alternatives? What might the consequences be? What is difficult here? Why?

2. It helps them to learn to analyse what is happening in classrooms.
By analysing and interpreting lessons in detail they can learn new ways of thinking about classroom events and new language and ideas. They need help in learning to see, some simple observation techniques, and discussion before and afterwards. After practice in analysing strategies in other peoples' teaching, they can try them in their own.

3. It offers a sense of the standards teachers set.
Learning what is appropriate, and when, is difficult. Teachers vary over their strictness. Different standards are appropriate on different occasions. Students need to reflect on the variations and commonalities across teachers and across age-ranges and abilities. They need to think about their own practice and how it relates to these.

4. It shows them different ways of doing things.
The focus here is usually teaching strategies. The follow-up needs to highlight things done and their appropriateness; the decisions made as a result of the unexpected; and the ways in which the student can try these things out.

5. It helps them to learn to monitor the progress of a lesson or pupils' learning.
This can bring home the importance of pacing/timing/flexibility/responding to individual needs.

6. It helps them identify things they don't understand, which can provide a basis for discussion with the teacher after the lesson.

Here the onus will be on the student to raise questions. Indeed, during the debriefing, students can be educated to raise useful questions that help them make sense of what they see and help teachers articulate what they have thought and done. Such questions include the following.

- How did you achieve ...?
- Could you explain why ...?
- What did you do in order to ...?
- Could you tell me more about ...?
- How did you know when to ...?

Haggar, Burn and McIntyre note that a successful discussion following a teacher being observed is one in which: 'the teacher did most of the talking; the teacher explained her/his actions...'; and the discussion revolved around the lesson. The student thus learns more than could be gained just from observation (Haggar, Burn and McIntyre (1993), Handout 4).

Being observed: how will mentors react?

Being observed is always a slightly uncomfortable experience, even when the observer has been engaged by the person to be observed and the specific purpose and focus has been agreed together as essentially a learning experience rather than an assessment. Under any other circumstances it is even less enjoyable and more judgemental. It can also tempt the person observed into offering an elaborate performance or demonstration which is more for the benefit of the observer than the pupils. Equally, the observer, by reacting overtly to events, can seriously affect the person observed, while unsympathetic body language from the observer can undermine even the most successful and confident of teachers. Again, the theories-in-use brought by students to the observation of teachers can mean that students have a very distorted view of events, ideas and intentions. It is also clear that in post-lesson discussions some students will voice ill-informed judgements about mentors' lessons. Mostly this will be the result of ignorance rather than malice, but, unless mentors take steps to ensure that students are versed in the kinds of positive questions to ask at this point (see above), it can provide teachers with frustrating situations.

TASK 5.3: POINTS FOR INVESTIGATION

1. Ask a colleague to come to observe your teaching. (Choose a lesson you want to find out about and negotiate a clear purpose and focus with the observer.)

2. Ask the observer to be sure to make some written notes during your teaching.

3. *Before* you discuss together what the observer has to share with you, write down a brief chronological narrative about your own feelings about being observed – starting with the observer's entry into the room.

4. What differences did being observed make to your planning; your performance; the pupils' behaviour?

5. What will you want to tell the observer to supplement what was visible in order that the observer better understands your lesson and your rationale for action?

6. Now discuss the observer's findings, respond to any questions and then share with him/her your answers to the above.

7. What have you learnt about being observed as a result of this?

8. How will your understanding affect the next occasion on which your are observed by a student?

9. How will it affect the next occasion on which you observe a student?

(iii)

The mentor observing the student

We are now in a position to summarise all that has been said and apply it to the mentor's observations of the student.

The importance of preparation

Overall, then, both observation as an approach, and its specific tools, need to be used as a part of a carefully considered and negotiated programme designed to aid consideration of the complex nature of professional practice, as well as to capture aspects of practical activities and to seek to improve them. Observation tells you only so much. Other data collection methods need to supplement it. It is behaviour oriented, but this does not always reveal thoughts and intentions. Careful preparation needs to be carried out by observer and observed *together*.

Before being observed with a class the student needs to have had a chance to get to know the class and to have tried out some of the approaches to be observed. Whether mentor or student is observed, the lesson preparation (or at least its intentions) need to have been talked through and the observer needs to understand how the individual lesson fits into the broader curriculum. The purpose of the observation, the focus for the observer, the time and place for the post-lesson discussion and the rough agenda for it also need to have been agreed. Decisions about all these will depend upon the purposes and focus for the observation, its place in the student's ITE programme, the needs of the pupils and the student's confidence.

The mentor has a distinct advantage over the college tutor as supervisor in these respects since there is more contact during a teaching practice between mentor and student than there can be between tutor and student, and thus there is (in theory) more time to discuss these matters. There are, however, also some disadvantages for the mentor in being known and treated by pupils as their teacher when she/he needs to be allowed to observe and assess the student and not be caught up in working with the class.

Planning the lesson and the observation

Clark makes the point that to understand the teachers' planning is to understand much about the teaching (Clark 1988, p.7). During preparation clear agreement/understanding about the following need to be established:

- the overall purposes and the specific purposes for observation
- how these purposes relate to the rest of the student's programme
- the intentions for the lesson and how it relates to the scheme
- the specific focus for the observation
- the appropriate observation procedures and strategies to be used

- their strengths and weaknesses

- what will be recorded and how

- how that record will be used

- when and where to discuss the lesson afterwards

- in what sorts of terms it will be discussed.

Being in the lesson

Mentors need to consider the following about the observation itself:

- when to enter the lesson (Should the mentor be in the room before the class starts?)

- where to sit in order to be least obvious to the student

- the frame of mind in which to approach the situation (Will the mentor observe with a positive mindset? Will he/she be willing to accept different ways of working from his/her own?)

- the nature of the mentor's relationship with the student and the pupils (How will the pupils know how to relate to the teacher-mentor?)

- how to operate during the lesson (Will he/she move round or stay still, help pupils or hold back?)

- the balance between observation and recording during the action of the lesson.

Mentors will also need to consider whether they wish to check out other data than that which they can observe passively. It is important to ensure that any incident which disturbs the mentor during the lesson does not colour the overall judgement of the lesson – particularly if the mentor is watching a student teaching pupils with whom she/he has a special relationship.

Recording observations and use of the records

The importance of recording data in a lesson observation is paramount. Some observation techniques carry with them a clear indication of how they record data. For example, the check-list approach usually has the items to be observed down the page with the number of occasions observed across it, and the ratings approach operates by recording the timing against the categories. In these cases the observer leaves the scene with only maps, ticks on sheets, or figures, all of which rapidly become meaningless once the context has been lost, and none of which offers very firm evidence once the meaning of the categories or the judgements of the observer in respect of the categories is challenged. What is lost is the rich texture of the human interaction. This also means that there is little to be gained by the student at the level of the quality of his/her work.

On the other hand, the unstructured, naturalistic approach can leave the observer unclear what to capture. Here a timed diary is often useful. And, of course, tape-recordings offer a further means of capturing the texture of the interaction. Here it is possible to share with the student afterwards a great deal of evidence, the very nature of which can often also prompt the student to recall what she/he was thinking or why she/he did or said something, and thus to unearth the bases of the professional judgements made.

One of the most useful techniques for getting to the heart of students' professional judgements is to focus on students' reflection-in-action. This can be used either generally in considering the whole lesson or specifically in looking at a critical incident within a lesson. It involves, *while observing*:

- writing only briefly about what seems to be happening

- simultaneously considering a range of possible explanations for what is happening

- seeking further perspectives on these reasons from within the lesson (by looking at pupils' work, asking pupils a few questions, looking at resources available, re-checking the lesson notes)

- and, in the light of these, generating in the observation notes a set of questions which will, in discussion afterwards, raise with the student some differing explanations for events and responses and some possible rationales which might underlie actions.

Some of these ideas are akin to the strategies for coaching suggested by Schön (see pp.86–7 above). During the post-lesson discussion the student's views about the practical and moral aspects of these can then be sought, and, if there is less time than expected for that discussion, the student still has access to the notes themselves which will enable him/her to go on thinking about (and even writing about) these matters. The following task seeks to offer experience of this.

TASK 5.4: POINTS FOR ACTION

1. Negotiate with a student to observe a part of his/her lesson, clarify the purpose as trying to investigate his/her reflection-in-action and your skills as a mentor. Clarify the focus as a particular (small) part of the lesson.

2. Observe as arranged, noting briefly on a time diary layout the main actions of the lesson.

3. Choose two or three key critical incidents where some action and response from teacher and/or pupils was noteworthy in some way, and focus on these, leaving the rest of the lesson to continue without your detailed attention (though you should stay in the lesson).

4. Think about the possible interpretations/explanations/rationales for what happened.

5. Consider whether you can collect any further perspectives on these events (as indicated above) and if so, do so.

6. Try writing down some questions that will unearth these different ways of seeing the events and that will lead the student to consider the practical and theoretical aspects of them (including the moral dimensions).

7. Raise these with the student after the lesson.

8. Consider what you have learnt as a result of this.

All of this makes for a very useful discussion of qualitative matters. But, of course, it prompts questions about debriefing, to which we must now turn. First, however, the following is offered as a framework to help mentors consider in detail their work in observing a student.

(iv)

A framework for reflection on classroom observation

The following offers a framework for the mentor, who has worked with a student in preparing for, carrying out and debriefing an observation, to enable him/her to review and reflect upon practice.

TASK 5.5: REFLECTING ON CLASSROOM OBSERVATION

A. Purpose of observation

1. What exactly was the purpose of your observation? (Did you have a clear intention?)

2. Was this intention clear to the student? (How much of it did the student shape?)

3. What exactly did you intend to focus on in the lesson in order to achieve that purpose?

4. Did you in fact focus on this? (If not, what did you do?)

B. Preparation

1. Had you seen (overseen?) the student's preparation?

2. Did you look at this before or during the lesson? (Was that significant?)

3. What were the student's intentions for the lesson?

4. What preparations had you made for the observation? (Were these sufficient?)

C. Evidence

1. What did you set out to watch for and why?

2. How long were you intending to observe for? (Did you? Why not?)

3. What *sort* of evidence or information were you collecting?

4. How were you going to use it?

5. How much evidence/information was necessary before you were sure you could come to conclusions?

126

6. How were you looking? (Wide focus? Specific? Checklist?)

7. Were you well positioned to see and hear teacher and pupils? (What would have been better?)

8. How did you record your observation? (What was the *format* of your field notes?)

7. How useful were these in your final conclusions?

D. Drawing conclusions

1. How have you responded to what happened in the lesson? Have you utilised a range of analysis, interpretation *and* appreciation?

2. How have you used your evidence during this process?

3. How have the lesson plans and the student's comments before and after the lesson affected your conclusions? (Why?)

4. What other interpretations might have been offered by other colleagues/pupils/parents? (How – if at all – might other valid views about 'good practice' have changed the overall conclusions about this lesson?)

5. How have you distinguished between what the student intended/did and what you yourself would have intended/done in this situation?

6. How have you distinguished between *fact and opinion* and recognised the relationship between observation and interpretation?

7. Against what standard were you observing?

8. Were you considering *achievement/potential*/both? (If both, how?)

9. What allowance did you make for the effect of your presence on the proceedings?

10. What else might you have taken account of before coming to conclusions?

11. Might you have been over-influenced by an incident/aspect of the lesson?

12. What have you used in evidence for your *final* conclusions?

13. Are you confident that you are using this evidence reasonably, honestly and validly?

E: Assessing the observation

1. What theories/beliefs/philosophies/ideas/values/views on 'good practice' influenced the student in planning and teaching the lesson?

2. What theories/beliefs/philosophies/ideas/values/views on 'good practice' influenced your observation of the lesson?

3. What would you say about the quality of your observation? (Why?)

4. What will you do differently another time? What will you investigate another time?

Further reading

Hopkins, D. (1985) *A teacher's guide to classroom research*. Milton Keynes: Open University Press.

Walker, R. (1985) *Doing classroom research: a handbook for teachers*. London: Methuen.

CHAPTER 6

Debriefing, Feedback, Critique and Reflection

Introduction

An informed and systematic discussion of action is necessary to elicit the meaning from the practical experience, as we saw in Chapter 3 above, and to enable the practice to be refined and improved. As Wade points out, some teacher educators believe that engaging in this reflective process may be the single most influential task of their work (see Wade 1994, p.231). Since most teachers who mentor ITE students will be involved in talking with the student after observing or being observed in a piece of practical work, this chapter attempts to offer some helpful frameworks for carrying out these duties.

First, however, the terms must be clarified. The state of the very language in which we discuss practice and various associated mentoring activities is a sign of how tentative and relatively under-developed is work on enabling students to learn through practice. This is true both within the teaching profession and across the caring professions generally. In ITE terms like 'debriefing', 'critique', 'feedback' are not standardised − occasionally even looser terms like 'lesson evaluation', 'lesson appraisal' or even 'lesson assessment' are used − and there are no broadly agreed frameworks for considering and discussing student practice (except the government competences, see Chapter 7 below). On two cross-profession research projects (Fish and Purr 1991; Fish, Twinn and Purr 1990 and 1991), we found that no two professions used the same term for this concept.

The word 'debriefing' in this book is used to signify the activity of talking with the student about practice that has been shared by both teacher (mentor) and student, in which either was the main actor and the other the main observer. It is, of course, also possible for students to operate with their peers in respect of debriefing and to develop self-assessment processes involving a debriefing approach (see Chapter 7 below). As Stengelhofen says:

> Peer feedback is also important in laying down the concept that it is part of professional work to be observed and evaluated by one's own colleagues.
> (Stengelhofen 1993, p.165)

'Debriefing', then, denotes a broad activity and is preferable to terms like 'critique' ('crit.') or 'feedback' because it is more neutral in tone, has more the sense of someone being helped to uncover what they know tacitly already, and fits more appropriately the discussion led by the student of the teacher's practice. Although the intention of feedback is to offer information to aid people in making adjustments to skills and the knowledge and emotional dimensions that affect them, I would argue that it is nonetheless essentially judgemental. Ende (1983, referred to in Stengelhofen 1993, p.154) suggests that 'feedback occurs when a student is offered insight into what she/he actually did' (and compares this to a ballet-dancer learning in front of a mirror). This, I believe, is a useful process, and ought to be part of any debriefing, but I do not see it as a separate category. I suspect that it does not necessarily further the student's learning if the insight is offered by the observer rather than emanating from the observed. The term 'critique', as we shall see below, I have reserved for one subset of debriefing activities.

(i)

What is involved in debriefing?

First, then, because there is no agreed coherent view of it available, I offer in the spirit of the reflective practitioner a *framework* for considering issues about debriefing, an essential requirement of which, as with all scholarly matters, is that it should be done systematically and with discipline. Research carried out across a range of professions shows that this is rarely the case (Fish and Purr 1991; Fish, Twinn and Purr 1990 and 1991). The following offers a summary of the kinds of issues that need to be considered in debriefing. The mentor's orientation to the TR or PA approach to professionalism will determine the character of the decisions made within each dimension.

A framework for considering debriefing

There are at least six dimensions to debriefing: the aims; the orientation; the mode; the pedagogic style; the format; and the nature and use of evidence. As McIntyre points out, debriefing (which he calls 'feedback') does different jobs at different stages in the student's development (McIntyre 1994, p.86). This means that each of these dimensions becomes more or less significant according to the mentor's professional judgement in the specific situation. The details of these dimensions are as follows.

Aims
The intentions of a debriefing after action are to help the student to elicit meaning from the action. The purpose and focus for the *observation* will already have been decided as preparation for the observation. But the reasons for offering a debriefing can still vary. Some views about what supervision (and especially debriefing) consist of have been recorded by Watkins. Amongst them are the following:

- assisting someone to reflect critically

- guiding and supporting

- supporting and building

- leading by example
  (Watkins 1992, p.104)

Stengelhofen offers the following additional aims of supervision:

- to lead the student towards independent practice

- to build the students' confidence in their own skills

- to facilitate behavioural change

- to help students to arrive at a complete view of the professional role as well as to attend to the detail within it.
  (Stengelhofen 1993, p.173)

But, as Lucas points out, in many supervisory situations there are likely to be conflicting aims for the mentor and resulting tensions for the student. He explores those problems which result from the mentor's conflicting aims of being a resource for the reflective student on the one hand and needing to offer the student new insights unavailable through reflection on the other; and of helping the student to learn at the same time as needing to assess. It is also possible that while the mentor is encouraging autonomous reflection, the result is that the student merely goes through the motions of reflection in order to please the supervisor (see Lucas 1991). The mentor needs to be aware of these possibilities and to be flexible in responding to them during debriefing.

Orientation

It is also worth asking about whether the general orientation of the debriefing is to improve practice and/or foster professional judgement (refine action), or facilitate deliberation about issues, or, if both, where the balance lies. Further, it is worth considering whether the focus of debriefing is going to be on the student's teaching or the pupils' learning. (It is generally the case that students take a longer time to focus on the needs of their pupils rather than on their own learning.)

Modes

I would suggest that there are four main modes of debriefing: a critique mode; a reflective mode; a formal assessment mode; and a self-assessment mode.

A **critique mode** offers 'a crit.' of the lesson. Here the lead observer picks out salient points of positive and negative aspects of the lesson and offers his/her own professional judgements about it and how the person observed might do better next time. In its best form 'critique' means, as it does of art critiques, an appreciation of the lesson. In its most instrumental form it might use a checklist of competences. (*This* activity is sometimes called 'feedback'.)

A **reflective mode** offers both observer and observed a means of exploring what happened during the lesson and of thinking about how it might have been perceived, why it was as it was, the theories that underlay the actions and how to improve next time. Here the person observed has the opportunity to examine and refine his/her *own* professional judgements.

The **formal assessment mode** offers an official judgement of the lesson against a set standard (now the list of competences). It is put on record. This assessment may be formative (during the practice) or summative (at the end of the practice). This latter is about passing or failing a student and acting as gate-keeper to the profession. (This aspect will be dealt with in detail in Chapter 7 below.)

The **self-assessment mode** offers a framework for the student to begin to take over the professional development role for him/herself.

Pedagogic style

Pedagogic style, broadly, is about the debriefer's teaching style. This involves either *telling* the student or *asking* him/her, and this in turn depends on whether the debriefer wants to demonstrate knowledge or lead the student to discover it; and whether the debriefer wants to do all the work or facilitate the student's self-assessment. Video and tape-recordings, however, can be useful as the bases of debriefing.

Format

The format of the debrief can be oral or written. Students usually look for *both*, and can be found in staffrooms comparing their written notes with those of other students – either in detail or in terms of overall parity of treatment. In both oral and written feedback the order of questions or comments and the tone of them are vital. The format of the written record depends crucially on the intention of the observation and the preferred (or prescribed) pedagogic style. The written basis can be discursive/descriptive writing (longhand or note form) or filled-in forms. Forms are inevitably reductionist, but might enable the occasional focus on a small part of a lesson. Where a form has been filled in by the mentor, its purpose, its role in the debriefing and its significance after the debriefing need to be very clear. Haggar *et al.* (1993) and Stengelhofen (1993) advocate forms as providing an objective basis for feedback. I would argue that they are no less subjective than any other records.

Nature and use of evidence

As indicated above (p.114), during debriefing there are two approaches to the utilisation of information collected during observation. On the one hand it is possible to offer it as evidence for critiques provided for the student; on the other it is useful as the basis for discussion with the student about a range of aspects of the practice. In the first case the information is treated as unproblematic, 'hard' evidence about the student's success in performance; in the second it is seen as much less certain and as a means of exploring ideas and the roots of practice.

Interpersonal skills and debriefing

There are some mentor training courses that seem to be made up solely of counselling skills on the grounds that the most difficult aspect of debriefing is talking to the student about issues that will not be comfortable for either party. Whilst I would argue that developing an understanding of the deeper aspects of ITE is a more major priority, I do not dismiss the importance of such matters – particularly since both in my own experience and in the research evidence it is clear that debriefing must take account of the emotional dimension. Students, for example, often attend more to the tone of voice than to the content of debriefing. And, in their role as assessors, some teachers have difficulty in pointing out students' weaknesses and in failing them if it is necessary. Stengelhofen refers to the useful work of Pickering (1987) in identifying ten behavioural skills that are associated with empathy and which are of importance in debriefing. These are:

> attending, acknowledging; restating, paraphrasing; reflecting; inter-preting; summarizing, synthesis; supportive questioning; giving feedback; supporting; checking perceptions; being quiet.
> (Stengelhofen 1993, p.161)

Again, of course, it is not the skills that are important but an understanding about the activities of mentoring and the consequent professional judgement about when, how, and why to use them.

The following rules of thumb for the interpersonal aspects of debriefing are based upon, but extended from the work of, Rowie Shaw (see Shaw 1992).

SOME USEFUL RULES OF THUMB FOR DEBRIEFING

1. Always be clear about and make sure the student is clear about the intention of the observation.

2. Always try to make the observation and debriefing a learning situation for the student. Be positive as a first step. Never give negative feedback in public settings. If you offer negative feedback, show how things can be improved. Be specific; offer alternatives. (Suggest a new small target that will lead to success.)

3. Work *with* a student not *on* him/her. Avoid a power struggle. Don't take control over the interaction – we are all learners. Avoid suggesting that there are simple right answers.

4. Don't tackle too many things at once – try to foster a sense of progress.

5. Get the comments and ideas from the student. Asking is usually better than telling.

6. Giving negative criticism or leading the student to focus on the things that did not work is sometimes important and should not be avoided. (It is tempting to avoid dealing with unsatisfactory work, but things will not improve without attention. There will come a time when it is too late to make your first negative comments.) Temper negative comments with praise, and help the student to see these as the growing points of the lesson. (Getting this balance right is a matter of professional judgement, wisdom and maturity.)

7. Use positive and warm non-verbal communication. Smile. Make eye contact. (Don't point, shout, threaten, put hands on hips. Don't be confrontational. *Listen* to the student.)

8. Use evidence from the lesson in as objective a way as possible. Stick to the facts presented in as neutral a way as possible. Use the evidence you have recorded (which may astonish the student) to provoke discussion.

9. Use open-ended questions, encourage frankness and share worries, uncertainties. Don't hide your reasons for questions or comments, or come at things too indirectly.

10. Always take account of as many dimensions of the lesson as possible (the intentions, the planning, the student's value-base, the student's experience, the different interpretation and perceptions of what has happened, the distinction between espoused theories and theories-in-use).

11. Your *own* different value base and different skills are only of indirect importance. You are not trying to get the student to be more like you, but to be more fully him/herself (within professional parameters).

12. Don't be thrown by your own strong reaction to any individual part of a lesson. Don't let it colour the whole debriefing.

13. If you are asking the student to do something new or different as a result of the debriefing, be sure she/he understands what it is you are saying. Follow up by asking the student to say what she/he will aim at, and what first steps she/he will take.

14. If you are offering judgements about something, make clear the basis of them.

15. If the student counter-attacks you, don't rise. Try to see it from his/her point of view. Show that you will consider what is said.

Explore it; clarify it. Illustrate your own position with simple facts and evidence from your notes. Show that you are neutral at the personal level — or even that you are positive about the student as a person.

16. Set clear intentions (targets?) for the next piece of work and even consider how the next observation will seek to help. *But: the most difficult cases are those clearly not succeeding but not recognising this.* There comes a time when you must be firm.

- You *must* have provided them with very clear and unambiguous assessments and goals to retrieve the situation.

- There must be evidence that you have done so, that the student understands the situation and recognises the deadlines.

- Keep careful notes of what you have said and what you have written, and how you have sought to help, advise, counsel and offer sheltered learning opportunities.

- There may come a time when you have to use these as evidence that you have pointed out the same things again and again and that the student has failed to meet the goals you have set again and again.

- Then you can:
  - describe the problem clearly to the failing student
  - ask for the reasons for it
  - listen sympathetically
  - indicate *unambiguously* the failure
  - offer help (tell them where to get it) in considering another career
  - check that they have personal support from friends/family (after some anger they may well be secretly relieved).

Problems in debriefing

A number of writers (for example, Stengelhofen 1993; Watkins 1992) point out dangers and problems associated with debriefing. They make the following sorts of points.

- Students tend to remember the negative rather than the positive – so good points need reinforcing.

- Students' views of what happened in the debriefing may be different from the mentor's.

- This may be because the student is not ready to accept the mentor's critique.

- Mentors can foist their presence and their views upon the learner (which is unhelpful).

- Mentors can offer apparently internally conflicting advice, or advice that conflicts with others in the practical setting, without giving time to look at these tensions and the reasons for them.

- Mentors can demotivate students when they step in and take over something in practice or in discussion and then complain that the student has not contributed.

- Mentors can provide too much supervisory presence.

- Mentors can fail to give reasonable notice of practical or debriefing sessions.

- Mentors can fail to warn students of problems until it is too late to put them right.

- Mentors sometimes will not let the student have full control and responsibility.

- Mentors can be resistant to a student's new ideas (and not even explain why).
  (See Stengelhofen 1993; Watkins 1992)

(ii)

Approaches to debriefing

Broadly there are two kinds of approach to debriefing, emanating from the two views of learning professional practice discussed above: the skills-based or competency-based approach, and reflective approaches emanating from the PA view. The following two examples each demonstrate one approach. They also, naturally, subscribe to very different views about the role of the mentor. At a deeper level, moreover, they reveal very different attitudes to the abilities of the teacher-mentor. These range from the view that the class teacher should simply offer a model to students and talk through what happened at a simple level, leaving the professional tutor and college tutor to debrief more deeply (see, for example, Dunne and Dunne 1993), to the view that the teacher 'is in a unique position in being able to provide precise feedback to individual students on all aspects of professional development' (Stengelhofen 1993, p.153).

Below I present two very different approaches to debriefing: first, the Exeter University 'levels of critique', and then my own work called 'strands of reflection', which is derived from cross-profession research (see Fish, Twinn and Purr 1991) and which is already being used considerably in a range of health and para-medical professions.

Levels of critique

While arguing that their approach to ITE is 'a model for the acquisition and development of competences ... that goes beyond performance and avoids a reductionist approach to professional training' (Harvard and Dunne 1992, p.35), the Exeter University primary PGCE Leverhume-funded research project, reported in Bennett and Carré (1993), offers what is arguably a clear example of the influence of the TR approach to ITE. This model extends also to mentoring, especially debriefing, and particularly shows how a course can atomise both the activities of teaching and of debriefing, and so restrict the roles of the teacher-mentor. It is a complex system and full justice cannot be done to it here. Readers are offered a flavour of the system here, but should not expect to be able to operate it without further information and the support of an ITE course team. The system assumes the availability of three kinds of personnel who will work with the student – a class teacher, a professional tutor and a college tutor – and is based on three models – a methodological model, a pedagogical model and a psychological model. It is the first two of these three models that are important here because they explain the differing debriefing roles of different kinds of mentors and how they were decided.

The pedagogical model adopted by this course is based on the notion that there are three aspects to the mentoring role: 'one concerned with meta-cognition; one with analysis; one with experiential learning'. These are 'assigned respectively to the supervisor, a school-based teacher-tutor, and the class teacher' (Dunne and Dunne 1993, p.121). The basic assumption is that teachers' classroom performance has to be modelled (watched and copied) in order for the student to gain competence. Another mentor (the professional tutor or teacher-tutor) subsequently assists students to learn further from this in relation to a set of criterial statements provided by the college. The college tutor then 'models' the process of thinking and planning beyond the current situation by addressing, with the student teacher, questions about how learning took place; about what was valuable; and what needed further development. Here the model of 'novice to expert' is seen as important, as is McIntyre's notion that enquiry into one's own practice is too difficult to be a central thrust of ITE.

The methodological model explains how the student is helped by the various parties to 'acquire' professional activity. A set of criteria for practice lies at the heart of all this (nine dimensions of teaching, each with eight levels of success). The thinking beneath this work is spelled out in Harvard and Dunne (1992). The detail is not able to be offered here, but the criteria are deliberately couched in problematic terms so as to provide a basis for negotiation by individuals in particular classrooms. They are used both to assess the students and to promote deliberation about learning.

The model of debriefing endemic to this work emerges from the following details. The class teacher acts as a model to aid entry to craft knowledge and is observed during a brief teaching episode (which is focussed on a specific 'dimension' to be learnt by the student). The teacher then observes the student, who practises what she/he has seen, and offers the student a critique of performance. (Here, then, 'debriefing' is about teacher giving feedback on classroom performance.) When the student, after practising further, can produce a good performance of this type, there is a collaborative planning session, and the student teaches and is formally assessed (see Harvard and Dunne 1992, p.40). 'Debriefing' here is about delivering an assessment. Later conference work with the teacher-tutor (or professional tutor), and subsequently with the college tutor, will 'raise to consciousness certain aspects of this craft knowledge, and thereby render it available for modification and deployment in related circumstances' (Dunne and Harvard 1993, p.122). This activity sounds very tutor-dominated and very far away from enabling the student to make personal meaning of the teaching activities and context.

What we seem to have here is a flavour of the TR training approach to learning to teach, which emphasises the atomising of the activities and personifies this fragmentation by ascribing differing roles to different mentors. Although the authors argue that the problematic aspects of teaching are given room, it seems that there is much that is prescriptive here. The sorts of debriefing allowed to the class teacher and the teacher-tutor seem to be as carefully prescribed, as is the focus. This approach operates what seems in *practice* to be a deficit model of teacher-mentors.

In contrast to this is the approach to debriefing that emphasises reflection on action as a means of understanding better and thus improving practice. I have previously highlighted a number of different approaches to reflection (Fish 1989, pp.76–80). The most important of these include the work of Boud, Keogh and Walker and that of William Pinar. The former offer a number of approaches to reflection and maintain that the goal of reconstructing experience is vital and that this will enable students to 'realize many things left undone, questions unasked and records incomplete' (Boud, Keogh and Walker 1985, p.10). Pinar, also in the reconstructionist tradition, argues for the importance of autobiography (Pinar 1986). Other publications, including Carr and Kemmis (1986) and Pollard and Tann (1987), emphasised self-assessment (see below, Chapter 7), while Griffiths and Tann (1992) offered a series of five levels of reflection for investigating personal theory. None of these, however, offer any detailed help for those seeking to debrief students on practice. By contrast, the following illustrates how a holistic approach to reflection might be supported by what is a *framework* of ideas.

'Strands of reflection': one framework for debriefing

The following framework was developed as a result of a small project which looked in detail at student/tutor discussions of practice in health visiting and teaching (Fish, Twinn and Purr 1990 and 1991). It is based loosely on the early work of Zeichner and Liston (1987). There are four strands (foci) for thinking about action that has taken place. But they are complementary and operate only together. They are not intended to be used separately; they are strands of one whole. They are: the factual; the retrospective; the substratum; the connective strand. Together they provide a holistic means of reflecting upon practice. They seek to aid interpretation of practice rather than analysis of it. The detail of each strand is as follows.

A. The factual strand
This is essentially descriptive and concerns itself with the learner-practitioner providing a narrative of the events and processes of the practical situation (what happened and what the learner-practitioner felt, thought and did about it). These are, of course, recalled

or reconstructed, but are thought through and presented as if the narrator is still within the situation. This strand stresses the immediate and apparently piecemeal nature of the practice.

It should be noted that recapturing or reconstructing a complex situation chronologically in this way is not always easy or straightforward. The mind/memory does not work like this. However, a disciplined attempt to re-live/reconstruct them, preferably soon after the event, will usually enable them to be ordered into a narrative. Such a process often enables the learner-practitioner to recognise for the first time what actually has happened. If, after hearing the student's version, the mentor offers his/her own, it establishes a genuinely shared basis from which further reflection can grow. (Many post-lesson discussions that do not begin with this 'ground-clearing' run into difficulties later as points of disagreement about what actually happened begin to emerge.)

Broadly there are three kinds of detail involved: setting the scene; telling the story; and pin-pointing the critical incidents. The following offers some tentative ways of teasing out what is involved in this strand.

1. **Setting the scene**
   Briefly describe the context of the practical situation, referring to the planning (including the intentions for the lesson) and the classroom setting.

2. **Telling the story**
   Give a chronological reconstruction of the facts (the events and processes) of the practical situation as it happened (was experienced) step by step.
   (What happened, how did the learner-practitioner think, feel and act, and why?)

3. **Pin-pointing the critical incidents**
   This is about focussing upon and considering critically the key moments of the story. Identify and describe any incidents which particularly caused surprise, seemed to offer scope for learning, made the learner-practitioner think twice. Say why the incident seemed 'critical'. Describe the resulting actions/thoughts/feelings.

B. The retrospective strand
This is concerned with looking back over the entire events and processes of the practice as a whole and seeing patterns and possibly new meanings in them. It stresses deliberately the retrospective nature

of the reflection and draws theory from the practice. It develops sensitivity and imagination by asking how others (other professionals like support teachers, parents in class, other adults present, pupils) involved in the piece of practice might have viewed it and felt about it as a whole. It thus encourages the habit of considering a range of perspectives on the practical work as a whole. It is also, to some extent, evaluatory − in that the success of what happened as a whole should be considered. Again, after listening to the student's attempts to think in this way, the mentor might offer further alternatives and stimulate further critical reflection about the issues raised, or introduce ideas that have not been considered by the student. The kinds of issues addressed within this strand would include:

- What main patterns are visible in the piece of practice as a whole?

- What overall logic drove the piece of practice as a whole?

- What were the overall aims/intentions/goals and were they achieved?

- How might others (other professionals/patients/clients/ children) involved in the practice see it overall?

- What new knowledge was discovered/invented?

- What might an analysis of the language in the interaction tell one?

- What patterns were there of reason and/or motive?

- How did the learner-practitioner see him/herself as operating overall within the practice?

- What patterns were there of critical incidents, failures, successes, emotions, frustrations, limitations, constraints and/or coercions?

C. The substratum strand

This is concerned with discovering and exploring the assumptions, beliefs and value judgements that underlie the events and the ideas which emerge in Strands A and B above, and does not merely involve superficial criticism of what happened in practice. It seeks to broaden the considerations out beyond the technicalities of the events (the 'how' of the situation, that is, the means) to a careful consideration of, or deliberation about, its intended goals (that is, its ends). This widening out is assisted by consideration of a range of perspectives from formal theory and other professionals' personal experience and theory.

This strand encourages professionals to tolerate the idea that a range of views exist about procedures and that there is no right answer. Here the mentor might interact at each point with the student, again offering further perspectives where possible. Some of the following provide examples of the kind of questions which may be asked.

- What customs, traditions, rituals, beliefs, dogmas and prejudices were brought to/endemic in the situation? Where did they come from?

- What basic assumptions, beliefs and values lie under the actions and decisions reported in earlier strands?

- What beliefs are emerging about knowledge and how it is gained and used?

- What ideas about theory and practice are implicit in the practice and the reflections upon it?

- What moral and ethical decisions were embedded in the student teacher's planning and in his/her actions in and reactions to the lesson?

- What beliefs and ideas lie under the kinds of evaluation and justification employed so far?

- What theories has the learner-practitioner proceeded upon?

D. The connective strand
This is concerned with how the practical and theoretical results of Strands A, B and C might be modified for use in future practice (or might or ought to relate to it) and with the practical implications of this. The information and understandings accrued via Strands A, B and C are now related to the wider world − that of other practical situations; the experiences, views, reflections, theorising and actions of other professionals; other personal theories of the student; and (via reading) that of formal theory. As a result of discussing these issues, the mentor might press the student to define a clear plan of action for the next lesson or targets for the next day's work. The following are amongst relevant issues.

- What has been learnt from this situation as a whole, how

has it related to past experiences, and how will it relate to future ones?

- How might both the thought and action specific to this practical situation be modified in the light of experience, of further thought and of further reading?

- What tentative further theories might be developed for future action?

- What implications do these reflections have for future practice?

Ways of using strands
It cannot be emphasised enough that these strands offer only a framework for reflection. The questions suggested are an attempt to give the kind of flavour of the issues to be considered within each broad strand. *They are NOT a TR set of questions to be tackled in a routinised way.* Equally, the term 'strands' is designed as a reminder that each is an element in an overall attempt to reflect upon practice and that no one strand is of use on its own.

However, it is my experience that the framework needs practice by both mentor and student before it yields a full picture. The danger here is perhaps that the professional tackles only the first two (easier) strands in the early stages. This would go against the spirit of the framework and, worse, would leave out those vital issues of underlying values and beliefs. In some ways, it is the substratum strand which probes issues which are most often ignored in evaluation and appraisal, but which are the real base from which practice is refined, because it is the area in which our practice is most challenged.

This framework, then, is a means of facilitating learning through practice via debriefing. It is an attempt to give coherence and shape to the post-lesson discussion which, as we have found in the original project (Fish *et al.* 1989), is often without shape and structure. It is also a means of investigating practice and of pin-pointing aspects of practice that further need investigating.

It might be useful to any professional practitioner who wishes to learn from a practical situation. Such a practitioner might be a student or a well-established professional. It might be of use in a simple piece of practice or for both student and supervisor in their own debriefing about their respective practices. It might be used by the student alone as a framework for thinking or writing a journal/diary. It is often best used, to start with, in partnership with someone else who is also seeking to investigate his/her practice. It might also be used as an alternative way of investigating a piece of practice that has already been considered by some other means (for example, self-appraisal).

TASK 6.1 POINTS FOR ACTION ASSOCIATED WITH DEBRIEFING

These activities are designed to be tackled in chronological order.

1. Write a critique of your most recent debriefing of a student (NQT or colleague) following an observation. Use the following questions to help you:

   - What aspects of your observations did you share with the student?

   - How many things have you highlighted for attention?

   - Did the student manage to set new targets?

   - What were the key differences between what you said to the student and what you wrote for the student? Why did they occur?

   - Did discussion with the student teach you something new about the lesson? (Did it cause you to change your mind about an aspect of it?)

   - What did you expect would happen during the debriefing and after it? (Did it?)
     Encourage the student to summarise your feedback session. Compare accounts.

2. Use 'Strands' on a lesson of your own, paying particular attention to Strands C and D; either talk it through with a colleague or write about it.

3. Watch a student's lesson (or video a student and sit with some colleagues to watch it). First, pin-point some issues about the lesson to which you would wish to alert the student. Then, using 'Strands', select the key questions, and/or devise your own based on 'Strands', that would be most helpful in getting the student observed to see for him/herself the important points you have highlighted. List these questions in the order in which you would use them with the student. (Where possible compare your ideas with a colleague's.)

4. Watch a student teach, making your own diary notes of key

events. Then, using 'Strands', explore with the student both the lesson and the Strands framework. (Perhaps then ask the questions suggested in the first task above.

Further reading

Boud, D., Keogh, R. and Walker, D. (1985) *Reflection: turning experience into learning*. London: Kogan Page.

Griffiths, M. and Tann, S. (1992) 'Using reflective practice to link personal and public theories' *Journal of Education for Teaching*, **18** (1), pp.69–84.

Pinar, W. (1986) '"Whole, bright, deep with understanding": issues in qualitative research and autobiographical method', in Taylor, P.H. (Ed.) (1986) *Recent developments in curriculum studies*. Windsor: NFER/Nelson, pp.3–18.

Wood, P. (1987) 'Life histories and teacher knowledge', in Smyth, J. (Ed.) (1987) *Educating teachers: changing the nature of pedagogical knowledge*. Lewes: Falmer Press, pp.121–35.

CHAPTER 7

Considering Competences and Assessing Professional Competence

Introduction

Mentors are now required, at the minimum, to take the lead in judging students' suitability to enter the teaching profession, and school-centred mentors will make such judgements alone. The assessment must be made by 'measuring' students against the government's list of competences, and mentors are required to keep track continualiy of students' progress. Further, the government intends, via the TTA, to produce a profile which teachers may be required to complete for student teachers who will take it with them through their careers (and which, it is to be hoped, will be based upon something more than competences). For these reasons the central focus of this chapter is on practical assessment. Section ii suggests some principles of procedure for assessing students against competences. Section iii looks at providing a more balanced assessment of the student teacher to supplement competency-based assessment, and proposes a holistic approach to the assessment of reflective practice. Section iv focusses briefly on the mentor as assessor. First, however, in Section i, as a prior concern, the problematic nature of assessment itself is probed, and some principles related to assessment are set out.

(i)

The problematic nature of assessment

Although the government, for its own purposes, portrays assessment as a simple matter, like all aspects of education, it is in fact complex and problematic. In order, as a reminder for mentors, to offer in a short space some flavour of its nature and of the inevitably conflicting principles that can be made to emerge from it, this section will begin with those aspects of assessment that mentors are most familiar with, namely pupil assessment, and move from there to consider the assessment of student teachers. Following this, it will then consider teacher appraisal and, in passing, will comment upon the relationship between the three aspects.

Pupil assessment, assessing student teachers and teacher appraisal

The following two contrasting approaches to pupil assessment attempt to demonstrate some of its conflicting concerns.

In an extreme version of what might be described as the training or delivery model of learning (which model currently exists in both the National Curriculum and in ITE), the trainer is responsible for 'delivering' the learning, and assessing whether or how well it has been received by the pupil. Such assessment is most often summative, offering a summary of the learning achieved at the end of the course, and formal, being a self-contained unit in an artificial or unfamiliar situation which happens outside, or after, the learning itself. It is 'applied' by the trainer to the learner. It is either norm-referenced (where the learner is compared against the standard of the group (or nation)), or criterion-referenced (where the learner is required to meet criteria already set down about what should be learnt). The purpose of such assessment is to assess (measure) the learner against a standard and to allow the trainer to check-up on the learner – usually on the learner's recall or skills acquisition – and to classify him/her on the basis of it.

The ubiquitous 'standards' (currently everywhere important) are created either on the basis of the norm for the group or on the basis of competences. But they are merely external reference points which at bottom are notional. Assessing pupils relies, in norm-referenced assessment, on the notion of an average performance of a group (the group size ultimately being arbitrary) and in criterion-referenced assessment on the basis of 'those aspects of performance which can be assessed in work activity ... or the learning programme which will result in an efficient performance' (Masefield 1989, p.30). This so-called 'task model' of standards provides a description of what the individual would have to do in order to demonstrate competence, but is in fact inadequate for all but the most basic of tasks (see Mitchell 1989).

Such learning is often short-term, is not owned by, and barely touches or stays with the learner. (Most of us have known examinations of this sort.) Although marking, which masquerades as absolute under the cover of exact numbers, is actually a very inexact science, assessment of this kind *appears* to be objective. This is because it is bureaucratically organised on a large scale (although in fact the scale mitigates against careful, detailed and individual sizing-up of the learner's understanding). Such assessment involves teacher (or examiner) marking a 'performance' which is visible and quantifiable, instead of focussing on long-term and in-depth understanding (which might be preferable, but is less visible and is notoriously difficult to make evident as the basis of formal assessments). Equally unattended to in this approach to assessment is the holistic view of the pupil as a human being with personality and emotions, interests and difficulties, strengths and weaknesses. There is no interest here in enabling the pupils to come to grips with self-knowledge, neither is there real concern to enable the learner to engage in self-assessment. The purpose of this approach to assessment is to divide up and label pupils for bureaucratic and political rather than for educational ends.

By stark contrast, but equally problematic, is the model of learning and assessment that places emphasis entirely on the processes of learning at the expense of visible outcomes and where assessment is formative (simply a tool to support learning), informal, and part of the day-to-day educational activity of the classroom. This approach is incompatible with our current national obsessions for empirical evidence, public standards and the comfort of certain knowledge and is of no use where categorising learners is necessary. It values the long-term nature of education, acknowledges the individual needs of the learner, and the subjectivity of marking, to the point where nothing tangible is recorded, assessment is merely continuous informal feedback to the learner and the emphasis is on the whole individual. No interest is taken in progress against national standards but only against the pupil's previous attainments (assessment is self-referenced, or 'ipsative', and is recorded in individual, student-centred profiles). However, the notion of capturing on paper 'the whole child' is itself not without problems (see Broadfoot 1986; Hitchcock 1989 and Law 1984). As Bridges *et al.* point out: 'many profile systems are based on the false assumption that knowledge, skills and attitudes demonstrated in one context can be generalised as context-free abilities' (Bridges *et al.* 1986, p.230; see also Stronach 1989 for further details of the problematic nature of pupil profiles).

Both of these two extremes, then, represent diverging and even conflicting trends in assessment and very different ways of valuing human beings. The one emphasises psychometric tests and the marking, labelling and categorising of individuals against a standard; the other attempts to nurture achievements and understanding, and capture and celebrate the personality of each learner. One focusses on specific behaviours as achievements; the other values the multi-faceted account of a complex individual. One records specific learning that has happened; the other sees assessment as a tool of educational development, ultimately providing for an autonomous self-knowing, self-assessing learner. As such, they enable us to make the following general statements and then highlight some liberal principles of pupil assessment.

First, then, we can say that assessment is a very powerful tool which can be used for a variety of ends and that it behoves educationalists to be aware of the moral as well as the educational dimensions of these uses. And second, we can argue that assessments whose methods and timing are inappropriate to the nature of what is being learnt, and to the needs of the teacher and the learners, can seriously distort both what is to be learnt and what has been achieved in learning.

From this we might argue for the following set of principles (which has been influenced by the work of Bridges *et al.* (1986)) and which we might wish to apply to all learners in an educational setting.

1. The purposes of assessment should be carefully considered. As well as enabling classification and categorisation of learners, it might be a useful tool *during* learning, assisting learners in gaining self-knowledge and the ability to self-assess; assisting teachers in adjusting subsequent teaching; and helping pupils to recognise the achievements they have secured.

2. Thus, any assessment procedures employed ought to assist — even maximise — the educational development of the learner, whatever other intentions they also fulfil.

3. Since a limited focus on performance in learning might distort what is recorded about pupil achievement, the use of multiple perspectives on learning events and situations, and the use of a variety of assessment tools, might be valuable.

4. Holistic judgements about learners, inferred from a wide range of evidence, are likely to be more useful in assisting later teaching and learning than the narrow judgements based only on measurable performance.

5. Checking assessment judgements against other knowledge,

including the learner's self-assessment, might increase the accuracy of that assessment.

If these are useful approaches to educational assessment, it seems reasonable on several counts to expect them to relate to the assessment of student teachers (since their work ought to be treated as educational and since their treatment ought (at least to some extent) to reflect the kinds of assessment activities that they will have learnt about and which they will be expected to operate in schools).

TASK 7.1: POINTS FOR ACTION AND REFLECTION

1. Choose a group of pupils, or perhaps two groups of different age-ranges, and investigate the range of different *forms* of assessment that they have undergone during a day/a week/a year/a Key Stage. What were the real purposes of these assessments? What values underlay them?

2. How do the above proposed principles of assessment relate to what happens in practice in your experience? Why?

3. Are there other principles you would wish to prioritise?

4. How does all of this link with your own practice and your own beliefs?

5. What is your school's policy on these matters? How do you relate to that?

While following broadly the same educational principles as those suitable for pupils, student teachers' assessment must also take account of the special nature of professional knowledge and of the necessary preparation and procedures which allow entry to a profession. Student teachers must be able to exercise practical knowledge. They must also be able to be assessed summatively and, if necessary, excluded from the profession. Assessment must fulfil a gate-keeping purpose. All this is what seems to have seduced governments to abandon an educational approach to passing students into the profession in favour of the superficially attractive but educationally flawed assessment based upon competences. Grace, writing in the mid-1980s, traced changes and highlighted the then current return to 'direct and visible procedures' of student assessment, and showed how so-called 'teacher incompetence' was placed by politicians at the centre of 'the education problem' (see Grace 1985, p.3).

The drawing up of competences as the criteria for beginning teachers portrays skills as the only concern, assumes a commonly agreed version of the good teacher, implies that assessing the performance of skills is a simple, objective matter, and erroneously suggests that skills are both unrelated to context and at the same time generic and generalisable to all contexts. In fact, as McIntyre points out in his discussion of the criterion-referenced assessment of teaching (written before the emergence of the government competences), the kind of assessment designed for student teachers crucially depends on how the activity of teaching is seen. For example, is it understood best as a set of personal characteristics, is it a skilled craft, a theory-based technology or a political activity (see McIntyre 1989, pp.64−5)? There is also a problem in applying pre-specified criteria to uncertain human interactions. He reminds us too that there is no agreed theory of competences from which to derive a list of requirements.

The performance of skills as the practical basis for entry to a profession is a seductive idea. The apparent advantages are that they lend themselves to clear statements about what learners should know, should be able to do or to demonstrate, and how and against what criteria they are assessed, and provide simple reporting to students, other mentors, colleagues and employers (which is particularly valuable when assessment is about to be handed over to busy teachers) (see Bullough and Gitlin 1994, p.71; Chown and Last 1993, p.16). They are also claimed to open up more flexible ways of learning via units and modules, although this is arguable. Further, using competences for assessment appears to improve basic skills in the short term (though at the expense of the long term); it is easily organised into a bureaucratic model for administrative purposes, thus apparently increasing efficiency; it appears to lead to objective assessment (which hides value-judgements); and is about improving the performance of basic skills (though at the expense of understanding the complexities of when and how to use them). Garland defends them stoutly. He argues that they 'ensure the maintenance of objective, reified standards' and that they *can* enable 'wider issues and processes' to be used, and can be a basis from which learner-centred approaches and learner autonomy can be developed (Garland 1994, pp.17−18). He also maintains that criteria of this sort are being adopted for most vocational qualifications in the Further Education sector and that plans for introduction of them into HE are well under way in the shape of General National Vocational Qualifications (GNVQs). He argues for processes to be enshrined as competences 'to ensure that ... personal and professional developments are identified as crucial' (Garland 1994, p.19). He seems unaware, however, of the philosophical distinction between competence and competences (see above, p.47).

The real problems, however, are that competences entirely 'fail to account for much of what teachers do and more importantly, *why* they do it' (Chown and Last 1993, p.15), and lead to 'serious difficulties in training and education' (Ashworth and Saxton 1990, p.3). Particularly they deny the importance of the nature of professional activity and of professional knowledge, the importance of and complexities of educational understanding, the nature of the teacher as a person, the importance of personality to success in teaching, and the activities of theorising, reflecting and learning during action. The competency-based approach also fails to identify whether the student is learning and refining practice as opposed to going through trained motions. And it shows no interest in the investigation of practice as a basis for improving practice. It is unable to recognise the essentially incomplete, uncertain and collaborative nature of professional activity, ignores professional judgement and risk-taking, and takes no account of the moral dimensions of education because it does not pursue reasons, motives, theories and values. Further, it takes no account of beginning teachers' own theories.

In addition, then, to the competences that are required to be assessed (and which in themselves *are* a very basic requirement), it is vital that students are assessed in ways which respond to these matters and which take account of other principles of assessment and the practicalities of operating assessment. And these same issues also hold for the assessment of NQTs (which arguably should be on the same basis as for ITE (see CNAA 1992a)) and for teacher appraisal.

Hartley traces back to Bentham the technocratic view of education out of which teacher appraisal has emerged. The assumptions of the technocratic approach (now so deeply embedded in our thinking that we barely notice them) include the assumptions that the social world can be standardised, made predictable and manipulated, and whose emphasis on performance, standards and competences invariably undervalue judgement (see Hartley 1992, p. 39.) Yet the conflicting nature of the emphasis on competences on the one hand and non-technocratic, non-judgemental and enquiry-based staff development on the other continues to unsettle the profession. (Many authors have argued for the staff development as opposed to the bureaucratic approach to appraisal, including Bridges *et al.* (1986), Winter (1989), Elliott (1989) and Holly (1989).) Even in the 1990s when teacher appraisal has become an accepted requirement, the reservations originally raised about it have not been resolved. As a result there are still tensions about the purposes of it (for professional development or for managerial control); about who shall be the appraiser; about the bases for appraisal; about who owns the information; and about who shall be made privy to it. Incidentally these issues have also been faced in HE where appraisal is also a requirement.

TASK 7.2: POINTS FOR ACTION AND REFLECTION

1. Choose a lesson (session) you have recently taught and list briefly, perhaps against a time entry, your own activities during the lesson.

2. Would you have done or said anything differently if there had been an appraiser observing and recording the lesson?

3. How might an appraiser, using a checklist of basic skills to be ticked, have recorded your work? What might have been missing from this record?

4. Were there any events in the lesson that someone observing but not discussing the lesson afterwards might have misunderstood?

5. If your 'teacher effectiveness' were to be generalised from that one lesson what would be said of you? How far is this a fair general picture?

6. If three sample lessons were observed, chosen at random from your work, would the generalisations from them about your teacher effectiveness be any fairer?

I have argued that assessment of student teachers (as of teachers) is not sensibly nor usefully attended to only by means of competences. However, they must be used during assessment, and we must now turn to how this may be achieved, before looking at wider approaches.

(ii)

Considering competences

During the early 1990s, competences have been intended to be the chief means of communicating assessment not only to the student teacher but also to other mentors and to employers. It is possible as the 1990s unfold that National Vocational Qualifications (NVQs), which are also based upon competences derived from task analysis, will be extended further and further to professional contexts and HE. It is to be hoped, however, given the demonstrable flaws in the thinking about competences for student teachers that, as with the extreme detail of the National Curriculum, sense will ultimately prevail, and they will be relegated to the minor role they really deserve. The following identifies some practical issues and indicates some possible principles of procedure for mentors who are required to operate via *Circulars 9/92* and *14/93*.

Using competences: some practical issues

It will be remembered that competence (in the singular) relates to the holistic approach to professional capacity which cannot be reduced to individual competences, while competency-based teacher education assumes that teaching can be atomised into individual skills (see above, pp.44–53). Hartley usefully summarises the assumptions and character of competency-based teacher education. The teacher is seen as the significant agent in causing intellectual development in the learner, and it is teacher's actions and transactions with learners that affect the rate and quality of learning. Competences therefore emphasise the role of the teacher and expect the observer to focus on this. Competences assume that the role of the teacher can be described in terms of specific, observable acts or behaviours and that these can be learnt and put into operation by intending teachers. Assessment is thus based upon performance of pre-specified and agreed competences seen in the 'field' setting. The focus of observation needs to be shared with the student in advance and levels of mastery of the behaviours are expected to be measured against a clear scale. Students should be instructed in these behaviours in advance of assessment and should be very clear about all the criteria used in assessment. Assessment should be based on performance, though knowledge 'may be taken into account' (see Hartley 1992, pp.43–4).

Some of the practical issues associated with this are as follows:

1. It is not clear how the competences relate together, nor whether stronger aspects of one may be allowed to compensate weaker aspects of another. (This is not a problem in more holistic assessments.)

2. Likewise there is no clear prioritisation of competences.

3. It is not clear what counts as evidence for 'passing' a competency. How often, for example, must a skill be seen, by how many different assessors, and in how many variable contexts, before it can be deemed 'mastered'?

4. How should you assess a student who can score as passable on all of the competences individually, but who is unable to establish long-term relationships with classes, who has no rapport with pupils, or who lacks the imagination or creativity to draw pupils to learn enthusiastically?

5. How does the assessor record the problems of a student who will learn to go through the motions of the required (known about and trained for) competences, but who does not really subscribe to them or clearly does not intend to use them once she/he has passed?

6. Competences (abilities) 'are not attributes of individuals which exist independently of the contexts in which they are realised. They are qualities of the relationship between the individual and the context in which she or he operates', and the achievements they signify 'depend upon the individual (a) understanding the context as an opportunity to exercise a certain ability and (b) understanding himself or herself as capable of realising that ability' (see Bridges *et al*. 1986, p.230).

7. Competences can be fairly assessed only by studying performance in a variety of contexts, and then generalisations about them should be 'the outcome of a comparative study of performance-in-context and not of a process of abstraction from context' (Bridges *et al*. 1986, p.230).

8. Assessment of performance should take account of the individual's personal interpretation of the context of his/her performance. It would be invalid to label a student incapable of a skill because of its absence if the student had 'read' the situation as not requiring it.

9. High quality performances are those which utilise those personal capacities and which call forth abilities which are appropriate to

and crucial for success in the given context, not ones which satisfy a pre-specified check-list of attributes of a good teacher.

Some suggested principles of procedure

The following principles of procedure are suggested as a guide:

1. Competences might be regarded as a basic requirement in two senses – as a base-level for assessing students and as one *part* of assessment.

2. This part of the assessment might be accepted as only attending to a very limited range of issues which may be supplemented in a range of ways. (Other ways of tapping understanding, of probing the moral concerns and of checking whether your interpretation of the 'facts' is accurate need to be found.) The third section of this chapter offers some help with this.

3. Careful consideration should be given to what is understood by the criteria required by government and any levels of criteria, measurements and other operational features suggested within the course. These ought to be agreed and understood in common across mentors, tutors and students.

4. The assessment operated should clearly assess what it sets out to assess, and not something quite other. For example, to 'train' students in a skill or competency, then help them to plan the lesson in which they will seek to use it and then to assess that lesson, might be to assess the student's ability to please the assessor and the assessor's ability to train the student. But it is unlikely to assess the ability to draw upon the skill intelligently in an unexpected but appropriate moment.

5. The purpose for assessment should be understood by all parties on each occasion. Such purposes might include the deliberate attempt by the mentor to check on abilities already well observed informally or to check on the absence of earlier problems originally made in non-assessment contexts.

6. The assessment should, wherever possible, be a learning experience. Equally, it should be clear to the student in which situations competences are being assessed and when she/he is free to experiment and take risks.

7. It is important to be systematic about observation and have a

clear idea of how broad a range of situations you will be seeking to observe the student in, what range of observation tools and data you will be drawing on and how many assessors should see him/her.

8. Systematic ways should be found of taking account of and recording clearly as part of the assessment the *context* in which the student was working.

9. Simple negative inferences should never be drawn from negative situations. For example, an individual's apparent failure to respond appropriately in a given context might stem from a different view of what was necessary or from self-doubt rather than actual lack of the competences. An important part of the data of performance assessment includes checking interpretations of context and understandings about self on the part of the student.

10. The list of competences can be used both formatively and summatively (during the practical teaching and at the end of it), but it is worth starting *not* with the words on the page but with the qualities and abilities of the student and filling in the list from these. In other words, the use of the list in a practical setting as an assessment tool is very limited, but it can be used as part of the reporting activity or as an agenda for discussion and negotiation.

11. What counts as evidence of competences needs to be carefully considered and what it is really evidence of needs to be clarified. (Avoid generalising from a single context. Success in one context may both look and be quite different from success in another. Some contexts are much easier to look good in than others. And the simple 'average' mark gained from seeing a range of contexts may not be a fair indication of the quality of the student.)

12. Achievements should be seen and reported as outcomes of the interaction between the context and the student.

13. Simply completing the list with numbers or ticks is virtually useless. The list can be used as a guide but comments need to be added. The notion of levels and measurements should be resisted if possible. Assessment on a pass/fail basis is less prone to disagreement. Especially seek to avoid putting everything as 'average and therefore three' on a one to five scale, which is often demanded in the attempt to 'profile competency'. (This

means producing a simple and highly reductionist document based solely on the given competences. A much more balanced form of profiling, where instead of starting with ideas about teaching the process of profiling begins with the human being involved, is discussed in the section below.)

It now remains to turn to the wider approach to assessment and to look at how reflective practice might be assessed.

(iii)

Assessing professional competence

In order to assess something we need to understand its nature. On the basis of all that has been said so far, I would wish to argue for a holistic view of the nature of professional competence and a recognition of a wider basis for the role of a teacher than that of the classroom deliverer which lies at the heart of government competences. (I use the word 'competence' here in David Carr's sense, see above, page 47.)

I suggest that good work in professional practice encompasses not *the* pre-specified list of individual competences that take no account of context, but a *repertoire* of skills, abilities, capacities, subject knowledge, personal attributes, personality and ability to work with other professionals, together with what determines their appropriate employment according to the context in which the professional is employed (namely flexibility, educational understanding, moral awareness and professional judgement). Further, the model of professionalism which espouses reflective practice (to which I subscribe) contributes some additional dimensions to the character of professional practice. It emphasises reflection (including ability to theorise during practice) and PA (the wisdom to 'read', the flexibility to react to and the ability to improvise in response to the demands of the specific context). It also values the ability, via reflection-in- and reflection-on-action, to refine practice, and the associated knowledge and ability to investigate practice. Indeed, Winter argues that 'professional workers in human affairs can only practise effectively and justly if they *learn* from the individual cases in which they are involved, since their expertise, as a body of knowledge, is always inadequate and incomplete with respect to its objects and purposes' (Winter 1989, p.192). Assessment thus ought to take account of this too.

Finally, I would suggest (contrary to many current views) that these aspects of professionalism are not a 'second level' of activity for the teacher to learn after she/he has mastered 'the' basic skills, but an integral part of what is to be learnt from the beginning of a course. As Russell argues, good work in professionalism *always* involves more than basic skills (see Russell 1989).

What I propose then is assessment which seeks evidence that student teachers have the ability and potential to operate as competent professionals and are able to ensure that the majority of pupils in their classes are engaged in an appropriate level of learning for the majority of the time across a range of varied contexts. This assessment should also respond to student teachers as complex and different individuals rather than demanding the same from all. This approach to assessment is therefore not concerned with the strengths and weaknesses of students' individual skills (except where one such clearly affects the overall competence or where a detailed analysis is needed in order to isolate and practise a skill for some reason).

An example of the *practical* differences in focus between this approach to assessment and the competency-based approach is captured in the following chart, devised originally to enable students to consider their own practice from different perspectives and to improve their self-assessment procedures. Here, the right-hand column offers examples of the kinds of objectives-focussed, competency-based, standard (rather closed) questions to be asked about a lesson; the left hand side suggests the sorts of questions that a reflective practitioner might ask given the purpose of both the lesson and the assessment of it. The two sides *do not relate to each other directly*, but are presented together to facilitate comparison. Although the questions are posed in a self-assessment form, they could also be used by an observer during a lesson.

Given all these issues, how then might reflective practice be assessed?

A holistic approach to assessing reflective practice

First, I suggest that the purpose in all ITE assessment should be to aid the educational development of the student as well as to fulfil the gate-keeping requirement. Secondly, influenced by the work of Shulman (1987) but going beyond his seven types of professional knowledge, I suggest nine aspects of professionalism to act as foci for assessment (that is, aspects that the mentor might actively look for). I also suggest four modes of assessment which describe the activities engaged in by the students and the mentor as a means

Table 7.1   Two approaches to assessment

Active reflective practice *(takes account of purpose and context)*	*Evaluating competences* *(in the light of lesson aims and context)*
What does my planning tell me about my values/beliefs/theories/moral stances and my expectations of the context?	**What did pupils learn?** What did pupils *do* to aid their understanding? How did I monitor them?
Why am I focussing on this piece of practice?	What do I know about every individual's learning?
What actually happened? (Several versions possible.) What critical incidents can I pinpoint? What do they tell me? How did I respond to pupils' queries/ comments? What does this tell me? Are there any significant patterns in what happened?	How do I know? What is my evidence? How did their work relate to their previous learning? How did their actual learning relate to my plan for their learning and for monitoring and assessing them?
What theories, values or beliefs underlie my practice? What role did improvisation play? What role did professional judgement play? What key decisions did I make during practice?	Did pupils understand the criteria for assessment? How will this affect my next planning? **What did I do?** Did I offer relevant, sound subject knowledge? How did I differentiate the work? How did I pace the work? Did I challenge pupils as needed? What were my assumed starting points – were they right? What opportunities did I exploit for pupils to learn core subjects?
What were their practical and moral bases? What theories and practices from other people will enlighten my under- standing of this? How can I systematically investigate this practice further? Are there any prescriptions about prac- tice that I should take account of? How does what happened link to previous and future practice?	How did I monitor their learning? Did I assess appropriately? Did I provide feedback? How did I manage the class? How was the class control? Did I explain, question, instruct efficiently? Did I use grouping appropriately (in the light of my aims)? **Resources** Were they appropriate and were they used appropriately? Was Information Technology used? (Should it have been?) **Aims and objectives/intentions** Did they take account of progression, continuity and balance?

(How will this affect the next plans?)

to assessment and which offer a range of possible processes of assessment for both mentor and student to operate. And I propose a different style of assessment from the quantification associated with measuring competences.

Throughout the course, the main purpose for assessment should be kept in mind, the individual student and the context should be taken account of, and the overall pattern of success (or failure) to enable pupils to learn appropriately should be seen as mattering most of all. The notion of 'repertoire' which is used here denotes the overall pattern of characteristics or skills which together make for overall success. No absolute order of priority is suggested.

The foci for assessment
The nine aspects of professionalism derive directly from the nature of professionalism suggested above. The sort of evidence that the mentor might seek about students consists of patterns of behaviour across a range of school as well as classroom contexts, at a level appropriate to a beginning teacher (or below that level if the student is not near the end of the course). The aspects are thus:

1. **the student's personal repertoire**: this includes personal characteristics; personality; general knowledge base; self-knowledge and ability to improve it. Included in these are: self-awareness; sensitivity to others; and ability to engage in balanced self-assessment. (McLaughlin, quoting Hare (1993) lists: distance, humility, courage, impartiality, open-mindedness, empathy, enthusiasm and imagination (McLaughlin 1994, p.159).)

2. **the student's subject or content knowledge base and associated curriculum knowledge**: this is knowledge about the balance, breadth and content of the school curriculum

3. **the student's skills/competences repertoire** (government requirement)

4. **the student's educational knowledge**: that is, knowledge of learners, learning, educational contexts and educational ends

5. **the student's educational understanding**: that is, pedagogical knowledge to enable the selection of appropriate teaching and learning strategies and moral awareness and ability to recognise the moral stance beneath decisions and actions

6. **the student's professional judgement**: that is, flexibility and

decision-making about when and how best to employ the personal and skills repertoire to obtain appropriate pupil learning in a given context

7. **the student's professional artistry**: that is, the wisdom to 'read' a situation, the ability to respond to it, and the capacity to improvise

8. **the student's capacity for professional collegiality**: that is, ability to work with a wide range of fellow professionals

9. **the student's capacity for professional development**: that is, the ability to theorise in practice and to recognise theories underlying own actions; awareness of own espoused theories and theories-in-use; ability to reflect on own practice; ability to learn through practice; ability to investigate own practice; ability to operate practitioner enquiry activities at a simple level within own classroom; ability to improve and refine practice and to recognise and work on mistakes.

Since the ultimate goal is the student's *self*-assessment, the capacity for self-knowledge and self-assessment should be both fostered and monitored as a part of almost all the assessment procedures adopted. Ways of enabling the student to gain self-knowledge (to know what she/he stands for, to clarify principles, ideals, to review personal attributes, to come to terms with uncertainties as well as certainties), ought to permeate all practical and dialectical aspects of the student's course. Opportunities for engaging in self-assessment of practical work should be built into all lesson planning and should also be fostered by a range of the modes of assessment discussed below. These modes, used together, will offer mentors useful evidence of the student's self-knowledge and capacity for self-assessment.

Modes of assessment
There is a range of activities which mentor and student can engage in in order to highlight these aspects of the student's professionalism. They are: observation by the mentor of the student's teaching; a range of kinds of discussion of practice observed; a range of student writing; and practical investigations of teaching and/or learning by the student.

Observation by the mentor under this holistic approach is a different activity from that in competency-based assessment. Here, the mentor is not present in the classroom to measure, count and record performance in 'objective' terms 'for the record's sake', but as one who shares the practical experience, in order to seek to make sense of it and to see how to help the student to make sense of it afterwards (or perhaps to collect information about an aspect of it for the student). As Garland reminds us, 'agreement needs to be reached between tutors and student-teachers' about what evidence is needed, how it will be collected and how presented (Garland 1994, p.21). Hanson offers an interesting perspective on what he calls the teacher's moral style by looking at tone of voice and body language in the teacher's responses to pupils and what pupils (and observing mentor) can learn from it about the teacher's values (see Hanson 1993).

Discussion with the student will enable sense to be made of observation and will allow the mentor to draw the student to theorise about or reflect upon it, to enable the student to investigate it or to make sense of student's written work about it. Discussion can take a number of forms, most of which involve the student in reflection upon practice. (Strands of Reflection (see above, pp.139–44) might be of use here, or the questions above; as might also a detailed focus on critical incidents in order to investigate moral awareness, ability to theorise, the success of improvisation or other aspects of PA.) See Tripp (1993) for extensive details on the use of critical incidents. For an important distinction between dialogue and negotiation in discussing the mentor's assessment of the student, see James (1989). For detailed examples of some kinds of discussions about practice that education tutors engage in with student teachers, and the sorts of strategies as that they use, see Fish (1995).

Students' writing can also give a clear idea of how they make sense of practice, reflect and theorise. Such writing generally takes one or more of six key forms. Of these the most familiar are the *essay* (see below) and the *teaching practice file* (which offers the detail of lesson planning and execution and records of pupil assessment and which has retained its basic shape over many years, but which today often provides additional important evidence of the student's reflection on practice.) Other, more recently created, written forms include *portfolios* and *profiles* (see below) and *reflective diaries and/or journals* (which often supplement the teaching practice file or are spread over an entire one-year course as a means of making sense of the course as a whole, which follow guidelines devised as part of the course and which may be assessed against criteria set out in the course document).

The important dimension of **investigating practice** is supported and can be assessed via *reflective/investigative essays*, where the processes of investigation provide a means of learning about school-wide and profession-wide issues, and for which mentors may now be asked to help provide data, to tutor and to mark. These are a major item of evidence about the student's abilities to investigate practice. Investigating practice can also be part of practical work in the classroom to which the mentor contributes. Haggar, Burn and McIntyre (1993, p.98), for example, show how mentors can be asked by students to collect specific data on a lesson as part of this process. Devising the observation strategies and foci for the mentor provides both a useful professional challenge to the student and evidence for the mentor of the level of the student's thinking about investigating practice.

There is much that could be said about portfolios and profiles, and they are clearly important for assessment of reflective practice. First, it is important to be clear about the distinctions between them.

A **portfolio** is a collection of evidence/data on the writer's professional development. It is about self-evaluation. It is educational rather than administrative. It helps the writer to be reflective about professional practice. It is a means whereby the learner constructs his/her personal understandings. It is a learning tool. Some would wish to maintain that the portfolio is essentially a private document, owned by the writer and in which the writer can be free to explore and comment about professional things without fear of them being made public. A portfolio needs to be constructed over a reasonable period of time. Some argue that having a 'critical friend' helps these reflective processes. A critical friend is one who will listen and reflect back to you the ideas, points, comments you make and help you to become clearer about what you are saying. A mentor might well operate as a critical friend. The role is not easily compatible with that of formal assessor, however, and some courses set up pairs of students who work together in this way. However, the quality of what a student as critical friend can offer is variable, though some courses try to structure the roles so that even weaker students can be of some use to their colleagues. Some, however, say: 'With a critical friend who needs enemies?'

In contrast with the portfolio, a **profile** is a summary or documentary history of a person's professional development. CNAA (1992b) defines a profile as a document which 'records student developments and or achievements gained either within the academic setting or workplace ... which provides the framework for teaching, learning and the assessment process by means of explicit learning objectives'. In this sense it fits with competency-based assessment. Used *retrospectively*, however, a profile becomes a different document. Then its content is often dictated by and drawn upon for evidence for use in a portfolio (reflective diary, journal or TP file). As a result, it can reflect the personal and professional progress of the individual and can offer a useful means of assessing reflective practice and professional competence. As such, it usually identifies some patterns, themes, philosophies, theories, ideals. Some would argue that the profile is the public side of the portfolio. It might also include a curriculum vitae, but it is usually more than a means of preparing documents for a job application. It should enable students to take the longer view of their career choice, to register the quality of their professionalism and to develop a professional philosophy of their own.

All these things provide important access to many of the aspects of professionalism that the mentor is trying to assess. The work of Holly (1984 and 1989) and of Squirrell *et al.* (1990) gives further details of the use of portfolios, diaries, journals and profiles. CNAA documents argued for the coherence between student and NQT profiling, but also reported that the Scottish experience of profiling (well ahead of the English scene) shows that 'discontinuity exists in assessment practices between initial training and the probationary period despite the profiling system' (CNAA 1992c, p.25).

Work on profiling for ITE has only begun in earnest since about 1992. Since then various studies of the introduction of profiles have been published, most of them based upon competences – but many going quickly beyond them. Examples include the following work: that of Ward and Richie (1994), in profiling students' progress in a Science Professional Studies component in a BA/BSc/ QTS course at Bath College of HE; of Vaughan (1992) on profiling IT across all ITT courses at Worcester College of HE; and of Davies (1993), profiling PGCE social studies students at York University. Of these, Ward and Richie's work is based on competences but emphasises processes (including reflection, critical analysis, target setting and action planning) as more important than the profile document itself. They pinpoint the need for considerable time to teach students how to operate the profiles. Davies' work, in contrast, eschews checklists and shows that there is a need for negotiation between tutor and student and a need for a range of assessments in addition to the profile and some tension between competences and personal qualities. He very usefully offers a flavour of the complex debates ensuing about profiling and its relationship with competences. Of the three examples, Vaughan's work was the earliest (pre-dating the official announcement of competences) and the most interesting in that it operated within a reflective practitioner philosophy and was not aimed at assessment but at students recording their experiences, identifying abilities and acting on the knowledge.

She indicates some interesting tensions between the students' use of the profile, the tutors' use in monitoring permeation and registering their own responsibilities in respect of IT, and the management demand that it should be of use in providing 'precise information relating to the quantity and quality of information technology provision in a form which could be quickly collated and analysed' (Vaughan 1992, p.166). Clearly, much more work will need to be reported on profiling for ITE as the 1990s continue, including issues about how the profile assessment should be recorded (the style of assessment).

The style of assessment
Instead of assessing students by means of grades, figures and levels, I suggest (as a means of assessing the other eight aspects of professionalism that are not taken account of by competency-based assessment) a return to the style of assessment that is in keeping with a holistic approach. Accordingly, and given that it is overall repertoires that are being assessed here, I suggest that for each aspect or focus, students are simply offered an overall pass or fail (with only the fail student being offered an analysis of the detail in order to have the chance to work on the issues necessary). But I would argue for the overall assessment in each focus to be based upon evidence of development throughout the teaching period (the student to be responsible for presenting this evidence), and scrutiny of the student in at least three of the four modes of assessment outlined above, and on the basis of the judgement of at least three professionals. This should not mean more than keeping careful records of these wider issues at the same time as recording assessments of competences already being carried out.

(iv)

The mentor, professional judgement and quality assessment

It remains to note that, in all of this, the mentor will be exercising many of these very attributes and aspects of professionalism that are being sought of the student, perhaps particularly since assessment has not until recently been part of mentors' experiences and will require processes, understanding and professional judgements that have not hitherto been exercised in this way. For example, there is some danger of conflict between the assessment and the advisory role; the mentor will need to be able to justify assessments, engage in a range of different sorts of discussions (reflective, evaluatory, justificatory); there will be issues about switching between the unequal power relationship between student and assessor and critical friend (see Lucas 1991). These will require a range of negotiation skills. There may be problems with students who seek to discover and fulfil the supervisor's agenda as protection against problems of their own being discovered. There will be students who are challenged to stretch to their best by the mentor's presence and those who find the presence of another in the classroom a hindrance to achieving potential. All these will need to be discerned by the mentor and will provide many opportunities for the exercise of mentors' professional judgement and PA. And, of course, there will be the inevitable need to provide a good professional model (in the general sense) of the reflective, investigative practitioner. Thus, as Smith and Alred declare in an article aptly entitled, 'The impersonation of wisdom', an important aspect of the mentor's knowledge is self-knowledge because 'the qualities that the mentor needs are distinct and unusual, complex and rooted in the kind of person he or she is, not simply the attributes that they have' (Smith and Alred 1993, p.112).

And, as if this were not enough, there are more advanced techniques and wider issues to which the mentor will also need to attend, as we shall see in the final part of this book.

Further reading

Davies, I. (1993) 'Using profiling in initial teacher education: key issues arising from experience' *Journal of Further and Higher Education*, **17** (2), pp.27–39.

Garland, P. (1994) 'Using competence-based assessment positively on Certificate of Education programmes' *Journal of Further and Higher Education*, **18** (2), pp.16–22.

Holly, M. (1984) *Keeping a personal-professional journal*. Geelong: Deakin University.

Holly, M. (1989) 'Perspectives on teacher appraisal and professional development', in Simons, H. and Elliott, J. (Eds) (1989) *Rethinking appraisal and assessment*. Milton Keynes: Open University Press, pp.100–18.

Smith, R. and Alred, G. (1993) 'The impersonation of wisdom', in McIntyre, D., Haggar, H. and Wilkin, M. (Eds) (1993) *Mentoring: perspectives on school-based teacher education*. London: Kogan Page, pp.103–16.

Stronach, I. (1989) 'A critique of the "new assessment": from currency to carnival', in Simons, H. and Elliott, J. (Eds) (1989) *Rethinking appraisal and assessment*. Milton Keynes: Open University Press, pp.161–79.

Part 3

Quality Mentoring:
The Wider Responsibilities

CHAPTER 8

Wider Perspectives and Advanced Techniques

Wider perspectives

The intellectually impoverished TR view of ITE, which is interested only in skills, denies the existence of the wider *issues* of professional development, just as it also ignores the significance of theory. It emphasises only an increasing mastery of predetermined classroom delivery tools, together with knowledge about and experience of the further responsibilities involved in delivering the National Curriculum and in fulfilling the statutory requirements of *School teachers' pay and conditions* (DES 1987). Since, in the TR view, these skills and responsibilities are all unproblematic, it is held that there is no need to seek further perspectives on them.

But it has already been argued that the mentor's role is to induct the student teacher not merely into skills but also into reflective practice in which understanding of educational issues, the exercise of professional judgement, and the investigation and refinement of practice play an important part since, as McLaughlin says, practice is 'inseparable from the critique of that practice through the critical study of general principles' (McLaughlin 1994, p.156). What, then, might be the necessary components and characteristics of an ITE programme that seeks to support such reflection and refinement of professional judgement and professional practice? If it claims to provide professional *education*, it must promote consideration of alternative perspectives at profession-wide level by means of a systematic programme of study. Such a programme must have a clear philosophical base, an intellectually defensible framework of content and processes, must offer coherence and progression and must have some sense of the conditions and resources necessary for promoting student teachers' learning about school-wide and profession-wide issues and practices. Only by this means will appropriate personal and intellectual characteristics be developed and quality forms of reflection be fostered. Only in these ways can be nurtured those thoughtful and informed teachers our children deserve.

The final part of this book seeks to consider these wider issues to which mentors will need to be able to offer students access via practice and discussion. This chapter will pursue further a philosophical basis for the inclusion of wider perspectives, and some possible frameworks and processes that might inform such work with students, together with a view about some conditions necessary for student teachers to learn about them. The final chapter will look at some associated wider demands on the mentor, including course design for ITE and associated quality assurance issues. First, however, the reasons for considering the wider issues need to be rehearsed.

Beyond classroom skills: a rationale for professional education

The arguments for engaging students in working at matters beyond classroom skills are discussed as follows.

Skills alone provide no basis for professional activity since training in skills offers no insight into when, why and how to use them, and teaching is not an activity for which processes and outcomes can be predetermined. Equally, although the work of one school 'as a whole' can provide a student teacher with a vast range of perspectives on the work of teaching, focussing on one way of doing things (or even two or three) would not provide adequate preparation to join a profession. This is, of course, not to deny that experience in individual schools can show how teachers' work is 'dependent on and shaped by schools as organizations' and can lay bare 'the various implications, for ... teachers, of the pressures and demands on schools from the wider society' (McIntyre, Haggar and Burn 1994, p.48). But it cannot do justice to the complexities of these matters, and facing such complexities cannot be left until later in the teacher's career because they will raise their heads even from the start.

In fact, training which emphasises the practical and focusses on the highly individual context and on entirely specific – even idiosyncratic – expertise, faces some very difficult questions about its educational value, generalisability, relevance and significance in producing broadly educated professional teachers whose preparation has equipped them to operate in different conditions and at different times. And if that training takes place exclusively in a range of schools, *without* the benefit of distance from schooling and without the opportunity and appropriate amount of time to consider the broad practices, the conflicting traditions, the range of alternatives embedded in them and how all these relate to the personal beliefs and values held by the student teacher, then those questions become not simply difficult to face – they become impossible. Then, there is no access to broader educational understanding, no chance to review assumptions (either those of the placement school or of the student) and no chance to develop a broadly informed critical approach to practice. In other words, school-centred training may provide some skills, and some contextual understanding, but it is very likely to provide only highly partisan knowledge, and almost no purchase at all on how to operate at other times and in other places. It simply cannot attend to enough alternative views of, and conflicting traditions of, practice, enough decontextualised deliberation about practice, enough principled understanding of education, or enough exposure to educational theoretical perspectives to foster informed critical understanding.

Equally, however, reflection on practice is not, of itself, necessarily of value *regardless* of its informing perspectives, procedures and outcomes. As McLaughlin reminds us, 'reflections can be more or less accurate, adequate, insightful, relevant, valid' (McLaughlin 1994, p.158). Reflection, used inappropriately or unsystematically can both undermine a student's practice and distort understanding. Jarvis, helpfully points out that *contemplation* can be characterised as 'the process of thinking about an experience and reaching a conclusion without reference to wider social reality' (Jarvis 1994, p.38). A way to avoid these problems is to be able to raise questions about reflection and its appropriate usage and in doing so to be able to draw upon the illuminations of a range of traditions of thought and research in ITE.

In other words, a principled, reflective approach to teaching (and to mentoring), *as an activity*, which involves consideration of a wide range of theoretical perspectives, is an important foundation for working as a professional teacher. The demands made by all this are illuminated by Michael Golby's useful clarification of the difference between the *nature* of an activity (like teaching in general or teaching, say, Maths) and the nature of specific and individual *practices* of the activity. Here, practice is the performance of a specific, local, individual activity: 'When we practise, we are always practising something, and what we are practising is an activity.' He argues that:

> an analysis of the nature of an activity will always be distinguishable from any specific and individual performances of the activity. Describing an activity provides a search for principles governing its conduct in terms of ends and means. Practices, by contrast to activities, are always individual and unique performances situated in a concrete context. Theory is the articulation of specific and individual performances ... with concepts addressing the ends and means of the activity engaged upon.
> (Golby 1981, p.222)

It should perhaps be noted that in later writing – quoted above (p.74) he uses the terms 'activity' and 'practice' the other way round. This does not, however, detract from the usefulness of the distinction being made. He adds:

> that clarification of the ends and means of particular practices is only possible through a process of comparison ... between an individual performance and the public meaning of an activity ...
> (Golby 1981, p.223)

He also makes the important point that theorising is a different activity from (though not autonomous from) the activity of practice. And this means that it needs to be practised too.

This must mean that even from the very beginning of practical teaching, wider issues are relevant and cannot be reserved until a later level of ITE or even INSET as writers like Furlong and McIntyre seem to have suggested. As McLaughlin argues, 'wider and more fundamental questions will inescapably arise, even in the early stages of training, and mentors should be aware of this and be prepared to deal with it' (McLaughlin 1994, p.156). This may be in contention with the ideas of Maynard and Furlong aimed at developing a model of how students learn along a continuum from apprentice to autonomous teacher, with associated changes in role for the mentor from model for student to critical friend and on to partnership teaching (lecture given by Furlong at the Cambridge mentoring conference March 1994). While the delineation of these roles is useful, I would rather wish to argue for a pragmatic use of them by the mentor in response to a more flexible view of students' learning.

All this also means that the preparation for mentoring – particularly quality mentoring – needs to appraise mentors of the intellectual traditions within which they aspire to work (that is, the traditions of critical thinking, alternative schools of thought, the roots of educational knowledge and the extensive body of research knowledge and research processes). It has been the intention of this publication to alert mentors to these at all points, both in the text and by offering further reading.

If, then, reflection is to be properly informed and systematic, and professional judgement is to be improved logically and morally, the understanding which informs them must be appropriately scholarly and embedded in a critical tradition, just as the practice which refines them must be part of a coherent programme. What, then, might the content of such a programme involve?

Access to broader understanding

The broader view of teaching and teachers' responsibilities presented in the 'Further professional development' subsection of the competences published in *Circulars 9/92* and *14/93*, and in the 'Professional duties' section of the *School teachers' pay and conditions document* (DES 1987), provide unproblematic views of teaching. For example, in *Circular 9/92*, the competences state in Clause 2.6 that newly qualified teachers should have 'acquired in initial training *the* [italics mine] necessary foundation to develop: an understanding of the school as an institution and its place within the community' (Clause 2.6.1) and of 'a readiness to promote the moral and spiritual well-being of pupils' (Clause 2.6.8). And the 'professional duties' of teachers are listed in the neutral language of bureaucracy as activities to be performed: planning, assessing, recording, etc. (DES 1987, pp.23–4).

By comparison, teacher educators who have attempted to sketch the content necessary to prepare a professional teacher have used very different language. For example, McIntyre, Haggar and Burn suggest that student teachers should use the school:

> as a starting-point for their broader professional education. How things are done in the school has to lead on to why these things are done, and why they are done that way; and that in turn has to lead on to questions about alternative practices and their relative merits, and to issues about the criteria being used, the evidence available, and the interests being served.
> (McIntyre, Haggar and Burn 1994, p.49)

However, in all this, they rather gloss over the need for time, appropriate space and expert guidance in enabling traditional conceptual frameworks about teaching and learning to be encountered and individual understanding to be matured. And they do not distinguish the different sorts of activities involved in turning from the practical activities and their implications to a consideration of their theoretical roots.

Nance and Fawns by contrast present the following questions to serve as an agenda of fundamental issues to be addressed:

- What are the different approaches to teaching?

- How do human beings learn?

- What should be the aims of education?

- In what ways does the school as a social institution serve our ideals and in what way does our social structure constrain us?

- What moral obligations do teachers share with their colleagues and educators?

They also point out that there is a great need for teachers to acquire 'the language and the concepts of education, the background history, basic theoretical frameworks, central ideas, and common pedagogical knowledge and traditions' and argue that this is still the role of education studies (see Nance and Fawns 1993, p.169).

A similar set of values seems to underlie Michael Golby's paper 'Mentorship: a Professional Model'. Here, he argues that 'activities in a particular school must be understood as part of a broad social practice. Such practice is not purely individual but part of a set of internally conflicting traditions'. He adds the following:

- This broader understanding can be thought of as a review of assumptions underlying practice.

- These assumptions are to do with the following: aims; the view of teaching; learning and assessment adopted; community and wider social and political demands; and school organisation and management.

- A curriculum for school-based teacher education is therefore necessary which will augment practical teaching with a thorough analysis of its more general import.
  (Golby 1993b, p.3)

The following task is designed to encourage mentors to relate what has been said so far to their own practice, experience and theoretical frameworks.

TASK 8.1: POINTS FOR CONSIDERATION

1. Select an occasion on which you have recently carried out a formal assessment with a group of pupils.

2. Jot down the details of the assessment, the criteria, the marking scheme, the key activities you engaged in and the key decisions you made during preparation, execution and feedback.

3. Say why you operated as you did, how else you might have, and rehearse the relative merits of these alternatives.

4. Whose interests were served by the decisions you made and the practices you employed?

5. What principles govern this sort of assessment in terms of means and ends? What theoretical perspectives enlighten it? What views of teaching and learning does it adopt? What are the expectations of the school and community in respect of this sort of assessment? How do school organisation and management relate to it? Why? And how did your particular practice relate to all this?

6. The chapter on assessment above may have helped you in this activity. How would you tackle other issues like group work, teaching style, learning, and personal, social and moral education?

It may now be clear that some of these questions require different sorts of attention if the student teacher is to be properly initiated into them. Some are focussed upon purely practical alternatives; some raise important ideas; some raise moral and philosophical issues. It may not be surprising, then, that to learn to handle such matters, students actually need the help of different experts and the exposure to thinking from different traditions, as well as experiences in different situations. It even suggests that learning to reflect on practice in a school discussion group may be a different activity − a different dimension of reflection − from reflection in an HE seminar room. This is illustrated in considerable detail in Fish (1995). McLaughlin also very strongly makes the point that:

> there is an important difference between the sort of critical reflection which takes place in a university seminar, where students can discuss matters in the abstract, and that which takes place in the context

of a particular school. In the latter it may be difficult to separate judgement and criticism of (say) teaching strategies and policies from judgement and criticism of the particular members of staff responsible for them. The possibility of the inhibition of critical reflection in school by factors of diplomacy and embarrassment is one which mentors must confront.
(McLaughlin 1994, p.159)

We have considered the rationale and possible content of the students' initiation into wider perspectives and are now left to consider how the work of the mentor and the tutor might foster this, and in particular what processes might be used to enable students to move between the particular and the general – the practices and the nature of the activity practised. Such matters might also give us a conceptual basis upon which to reconsider the distinctive, complementary and collaborative work of mentors and tutors.

Gaining access: advanced techniques for mentor and tutor

It has been demonstrated that students need to see how work in one classroom links to whole-school and profession-wide issues. Permeating both of these there needs to be not only a variety of practical experiences but also some experience in the activities of theorising both in a practical setting and in a deliberative one with other adults and distanced from the demands of practice. (Indeed, this in itself provides preparation for those meetings with colleagues, parents and governors that are a part of the teacher's role.) As part of this, students need to be helped to recognise and accommodate to the tensions between the general and the particular, the idealised and 'the brute world', between practice which is intuitive and that for which there is a clear thought-through rationale. And they need to be helped – perhaps via assessment demands – to formulate their own theoretical positions and philosophies, construct their own sense of coherence and be aware of and clear about how it relates to the traditions of educational studies and Formal Theory.

All this would seem to call for the expertise of mentors and tutors in a variety of roles and combinations. The following offers some examples of strategies that might be used. None is new, but some have the potential to be considerably strengthened as a result of the teacher-partner having become a mentor with more direct responsibility and with properly acknowledged time to be involved. (However, this benefit would be negated if as a result the expertise of tutors was withdrawn.) Careful planning is not only necessary to ensure the usefulness of all the individual techniques described below, but also to provide a coherent programme within and between schools, and between schools and HEIs (see below, Chapter 9).

Partnership supervision
Partnership supervision envisages the student working only with a supervisor (this would now be a mentor). It is a form of clinical supervision, stemming from the work of Goldhammer (1969) and more recently expounded at length in Smyth (1986) for example. The example chosen to typify it is the now seminal article by Rudduck and Sigsworth (1985). Their work stemmed from a dissatisfaction with the power relationships in TP supervision and a desire to 'develop a relationship ... in which the negative impact of the tutor's cumulative power would be contained, so that his/her experience and expertise could be positively used by the student'. They drew up contracts to contain the authority of the tutor and particularly to ensure that the focus of the tutor's observation was defined by the student and not the tutor. The student proposed a focus by 'nominating one or more topics or problems which he/she would like to have feed-back on' (Rudduck and Sigsworth 1985, p.154). These ideas were clarified, and the nature of the evidence and how it might be gathered were also discussed by student and supervisor. They found that identifying the focus was itself an educative process, that the relationship of theory and practice was explored 'as a dynamic reality' (p.160) but that it showed how easily tutors reverted to being prescriptive. It also depends crucially on the knowledge and expertise of the one supervisor to operate at both the individual practice level and the deeper level of considering the nature of the activities of which the practice is part.

Since this approach offers what Mercer and Abbott call a student-centred or democratic approach to professional development, there is clearly mileage here for the student's thinking to be extended beyond the particular and beyond the practical technicalities of the lesson and to begin the process of self-assessment and greater autonomy (Mercer and Abbott 1989, p.141). But very careful thought needs to be given to these educational ends, in order to ensure that the technique properly supports them. Thought also needs to be given to the overall coherence and progression of the course programme in which this approach to practical teaching is embedded.

Co-operative teaching
Co-operative teaching also involves the student with one supervisor. Much has been written about collaborative and co-operative

teaching as a means of facilitating student-teachers' learning, and it is a popular activity with some mentors whose schools already have extensive traditions of co-operation and collaboration (see Burn 1992; Haggar, Burn and McIntyre 1993; Hatton 1985 and Wood 1991). Burn usefully characterises collaborative teaching as: 'any lesson that is jointly planned and jointly taught by a mentor ... and a beginning teacher' (Burn 1992, p.133). She points out that the degree of collaboration can vary greatly, with the student taking more or less responsibility. She also offers three important kinds of learning that are possible through collaborative teaching. These are: planning; specific classroom skills; and gaining access to teacher's craft knowledge. As a result of joint planning, she argues, the student can learn what the teacher takes account of. But, I would argue that in addition – if the supervisor is concerned to focus on such matters – the student can learn about a range of constraints, requirements and problems that can move the student's thinking from the particular to the general. It is a pity that in her conclusions (as in the summary of the benefits of collaborative teaching in Unit 4 of Haggar, Burn and McIntyre (1993, p.69)), she ignores the possibilities of moving the student on to deeper discussion and instead argues that collaborative teaching offers a sheltered approach to learning skills early in the course. There is room here for the development of a much more educational dimension to collaborative teaching.

The work of Wood indicates other ways of reaching deeper levels in using this technique, in a section on sharing action research with the student and on guiding the student to become reflective by means of 'developing curriculum collaboratively, questioning and collecting data around questions, video-taping and conducting action research projects' (Wood 1991, p.209). For example, she offers a useful set of questions around which to collect data – and out of which discussions will inevitably reach out from the specific classroom to wider perspectives. These questions include: How do we as teachers spend our time in classrooms? What areas of the classroom are and are not being used effectively? Here there is the idea that 'the responsibility of a cooperating teacher is to guide their [students'] reflection from issues of daily survival into areas of meaningful pedagogical concerns' (Wood 1991, p.210). There is, too, a clue here for ensuring coherence and progression both within the practical teaching and at whole-course level.

A double focus
The double-focus technique draws on the expertise of a tutor as well

as a mentor. It is aimed at students practising working with pupils at classroom level but at the same time (even from the beginning of a course) it raises students' eyes to the wider issues of teaching as an activity. It is rooted in ideas about triangulation first introduced in the Ford Teaching Project and highlighted by Grundy as representing three aspects of curriculum knowledge: the technical interest in skills as a product (seen here in the student's natural early focus and possibly the teacher's); the practical interest of concern with the wider understanding of the activity (seen here as the tutor's and the teacher's interest); and the emancipatory interest, aimed at thinking critically about the whole process, including the social construction of human society, as a means to becoming an autonomous operator (seen here as, possibly, the tutor's concern) (see Grundy 1987, pp.84–5). By drawing on both teacher and tutor to work with the student, it uses the teacher's expertise in knowing and working in the particular situation and the tutor's expertise in enabling students to discuss teaching as an activity and to raise their understanding of profession-wide issues to a level appropriate to university work. (Unlike the Exeter Scheme, however, it sees the teacher and tutor as working together with the student and without the rigid prescription of roles.) Though expensive in staff time at one level, it is also economic at another in that it can involve as many as twelve students in one classroom. (I have worked with as many as eighteen students sitting among a class of thirty-six pupils and not over dominating the room, and have used the technique successfully with both primary and secondary students and with pupils from Year 5 to Year 10 (see Fish 1989, pp.144–62).)

The central thrust of the work is that students engage with pupils in pairs or small groups within a lesson of no more than about an hour's length. The lesson is taught by the teacher (whose first responsibility is for the pupils' learning) and is part of the pupils' normal programme. The tutor (whose first responsibility is for the students' learning) works amongst the students. The students' work involves helping the pupils but also observing and considering a particular issue or focus which will be discussed immediately after the lesson by students, teacher and tutor. Teacher and tutor have planned guidelines for use in class and to aid discussion afterwards (gradually, as these weekly visits develop, students are involved in the planning). Before the lesson begins planning has involved meetings between tutor and teacher, and, on a separate occasion, tutor, teacher and students. The (properly lengthy, hour-long) discussion immediately following the lesson focusses upon the practical decisions and activities of the lesson and on the wider issues that students were already aware they would be discussing. This is widened further by brief reading about the nature of the activity that same evening and an associated diary entry for the day. The following day, back in the college, the students (together with the teacher if appropriate) engage in more rigorous critical reflections on the nature of the activities, informed by the reading and guided by the same tutor who also has expertise in the practice of theorising, has knowledge of useful theoretical perspectives and experience of practices in a range of schools. Coherence here is provided by an outline programme which focusses progressively from broader to more specific issues about teaching and learning and which requires the practical teaching to be interlinked with the college-based course. This, however, is not in the hierarchical and rigidly categorised way that appears to be characteristic of the Exeter scheme, but rather in a way which enables the partners to negotiate their contributions to the dialogue of the general and the particular in relationship to their interests and strengths.

Here, then, is a technique which maximises the key resources available to student teachers – namely the mentor and the tutor; the school and the college. A favourite term for the threesome is 'triad', and Gore (1991) offers some interesting images for the triad and the triangle in a lively article on improving supervision.

Investigating school-wide issues

Finally, there are approaches which foster students' understanding of wider issues, both whole-school and profession-wide, which are not based at all in the individual school classroom. These include: mentors offering more formal seminars (though these are best shaped on the principle of involving students actively rather than lecturing to them); mentors facilitating investigations of whole-school issues; and mentors generally using the naturally untidy and pragmatic nature of issues and happenings to raise matters which students can be asked to pursue further and report back upon.

McIntyre, Haggar and Burn offer examples of several possible school-based programmes for such school-wide considerations, though they do not interrelate the school programme with any college-based work (McIntyre, Haggar, and Burn 1994, pp.53–60). They do, however, make the point that HEI tutors can usefully be involved in school-based activities and are particularly useful in reviewing relevant research evidence, finding out about practices elsewhere and analysing various arguments by theorists and politicians (see McIntyre, Haggar and Burn 1994, p.61). And this returns us naturally to the point that the critical reflections away from the practicum also have an important role to play in preparing the student to enter the profession.

Perspectives beyond the practicum

The role of the education tutor in initiating the student into practical discourse, and the associated activities that take place in the HEI constitute a huge topic, which cannot be described adequately here, but which is the subject of a companion volume to this book. It must suffice to say at this stage, that just as the sheltered practicum is properly found in the school because this best enables students to be initiated into practice, to try out practices and to learn at first hand what practice is about; so the university is the appropriate sheltered arena for being initiated into educational understanding, to try out ideas and to find out about the nature of education and professionalism (see Fish 1995).

Further Reading

Burn, K. (1992) 'Collaborative teaching', in Wilkin, M. (Ed.) (1992) *Mentoring in schools*. London: Kogan Page.

Fish, D. (1989) *Learning through practice in initial teacher training*. London: Kogan Page.

Fish, D. (Ed.) (1995) *Quality learning for student teachers: university tutors' educational practices*. London: David Fulton.

Gore, J.M. (1991) 'Practising what we preach: action research and the supervision of student teachers', in Tabachnick, R. and Zeichner, K. (Eds) (1991) *Issues and practices in inquiry-oriented teacher education*. London: Falmer Press.

McIntyre, D., Haggar, H. and Burn, K. (1994) *The management of student teachers' learning*. London: Kogan Page.

Rudduck, J. and Sigsworth, A. (1985) 'Partnership supervision (or Goldhammer revisited)', in Hopkins, D. and Reid, K. (Eds) (1985) *Rethinking teacher education*. London: Croom Helm.

Wood, P. (1991) 'The cooperating teacher's role in nurturing reflective teaching', in Tabachnick, R. and Zeichner, K. (Eds) (1991) *Issues and practices in inquiry-oriented teacher education*. London: Falmer Press.

CHAPTER 9

Course Design, Quality Control and Quality Mentoring

Introduction

The government requires mentors to 'take the lead in' course design for ITE. McIntyre notes that most past problems related to ITE have resulted from 'lack of coherence ... lack of shared understandings ...lack of explicitness about who is doing what and why'. He draws attention to the solemn and vital responsibility of mentors in respect of course planning thus:

> for mentors to be effective teacher educators, they need to become co-planners of the programmes in which they are working, and to do that effectively they also need to become co-theorists about teacher education. The old problems will remain unless mentors accept such responsibilities for thinking about the nature of teaching expertise and how it can best be developed and how therefore ITE courses should operate.
> (McIntyre 1994, p.92)

To become a co-theorist in this way involves far more than offering an input into a planning meeting about how ITE ought to be conducted inside schools. To appreciate the context of planning the school programme means having a highly sophisticated understanding of issues in ITE − for example knowledge of recent developments in thinking and awareness of current debates about ITE − of which all that has appeared in (or been implicit in) the preceding pages of this book records only a small fraction, and in simplified form. It also involves being familiar with course design issues and procedures.

Course design for ITE is problematic. There are no simple answers, there can exist no single model. To create an ITE course under the new conditions and current climate will therefore take considerable effort and time. If handled well, it could serve to bring the partners in training closer together and act as a staff development exercise. This chapter seeks to aid that process by offering mentors something of the flavour of the ideas and arguments, conflicts and tensions that both do and must exist if ITE is to be an HE enterprise, and which provide the context for course design. Accordingly the first section of this chapter deals with course design issues; the second highlights the school-based programme and associated quality assurance matters; and the final section considers the implications for the school of quality mentoring.

(i)

Course design

Situational analysis is arguably the proper forerunner to detailed curriculum planning. The following therefore offers, as an essential background to detailed planning, an 'interpretation' of the complexities involved, which reaches beyond the more simplistic models of ITE offered earlier in this book. A reminder is then provided of alternative approaches to course design which, ironically but inevitably, reduce the real complexity to a form in which the ITE course can be documented and thus controlled so that quality can be 'assured' in the terms that our current climate demands.

Situational analysis

Examples of trends and tensions characteristic of ITE in the last decade of the twentieth century are here highlighted below via the voices of commentators who view the scene holistically and from a national or even international perspective.

Skilbeck, from the perspective of the European-wide Organisation for Economic Co-operation and Development, usefully provides a starting point by identifying a number of issues and problems that are currently affecting ITE throughout Europe, many of which are related to the tensions and difficulties found in all the faculties of the modern university (difficulties of recruiting suitably qualified and well motivated students, the nature and quality of research, the governance of professions, the relationship of teaching to research in the academic career, as well as the pressures of numbers and resources as university education moves from being an elite to becoming a universal system). In response to these, he argues, teacher education is engaged in continuous reconstruction which is 'of necessity, a critical, creative, reflective and, above all, continuous process of growth and renewal' (Skilbeck 1992, p.24). He points out a number of trends that are shaping or reshaping teachers' roles and that should be noted as part of any review of teacher education. He sees these 'universal trends' as follows:

1. **the scientific trend** which emphasises the value of and need for greater knowledge amongst teachers (knowledge of subject matter and of pedagogy)

2. **the professionalisation trend** which emphasises professional responsibility and accountability (notwithstanding some evidence of attempts at central control)

3. **the socio-economic trend** which emphasises the role of the teacher, regardless of subject specialism or level of operation, in achieving the social and economic goals of the national state

4. **the partnership trend** which emphasises the role of teacher as partner and co-operative worker.
   (See Skilbeck 1992, pp.25–6)

Through all of these trends, Skilbeck maintains, runs the significance of knowledge, including knowledge yielded by research. In the light of revolutionary changes to our culture wrought by research and technology, he argues, we now know knowledge to be fundamentally uncertain rather than settled; and the concept of teaching as transmission, and learning as the acquisition and assimilation of what is known and believed by others, as essentially out of date. Clark makes the parallel point that 'research on teacher thinking has made an empirical case that the practice of teaching is complex, uncertain and dilemma-riddled' (Clark 1988, p.10). This, Skilbeck argues, means *as a basic requirement*, developing in students critical-mindedness, interest in and capacity for reflective enquiry and an apprehension of the implications of the intellectual revolutions whereby absolutes and certainties of knowledge have been abandoned. With this apprehension, he argues, students will come naturally to see that research is no less than the systematisation of this reflective, critical spirit and its translation into public forms of inquiry. Students therefore also need to understand the goals, general procedures and organisation of research, and experience its activities and read its literature. Research, he suggests, is continuous with, and an extension of, reasoned debate (the construction of an argument, supporting it with evidence, logical trains of thought, the checking of data sources, and the drawing of valid conclusions). He makes the point that such processes are (or should be) a normal part of schooling and be well developed by the time pupils reach the end of secondary school. If they are not, teacher education must focus on them in the early part of the course. He also adds that of course teacher educators who are not themselves researchers and scholars, who do not read research literature, attend congresses and seminars and who do not systematically build into their courses the relevant research dimension, can hardly help students in these matters (see Skilbeck 1992 p.28).

Part of the difficulty of planning ITE, then, consists of finding a balance between what Hargreaves (1994) calls the transformative and reproductive intentions in ITE. In an article that argues that we should consider the interdependence of the reforms of schooling and of the school curriculum on the one hand and of ITE on the other, he explores what he terms some unintended outcomes of the government's interventions. In doing so he offers what might be fairly described as a speculative analysis of some signs he discerns of change. They might have significance for ITE course design, and though they are clearly speculative and not grounded in research, they certainly indicate the kind of thinking and sensitivity to signs that must characterise course designers.

He notes, for example, Pring's view that the authority of the teacher is coming to depend less on the teacher's knowledge than upon belonging to a social tradition which 'defines relationships, sets boundaries, establishes goals and purposes and resists intrusion from those who seek to subvert these values' (see Hargreaves 1994, p.424). Hargreaves dubs this shift in social tradition 'the new professionalism' and characterises it as developing new forms of (closer, more collaborative) relationship with colleagues, students, parents, involving more explicit negotiation of roles and responsibilities. He evidences the way individual teachers' work is set within school policies and the planning and implementation of them, and the focus on pupils' learning and institutional development which leads to more sophisticated models and practices of professional development. He concludes that: 'teachers are not merely working more cooperatively; they feel a stronger obligation towards and responsibility for their colleagues'. He argues that the evolution of this new professionalism can be charted in relation to nine trends, which include the following:

- **from hierarchies to teams:** in which, as a result of a more holistic view of the school because of the reforms, and the need for a vast range of functions to be carried out, everyone has a leadership role to play

- **from liaison to partnership:** in which the relationship between lecturers and mentor has changed, and where practising teachers will contribute more to design and planning of courses, be trained (which involves lecturers sharing their skills) and share in assessment, etc.

- **from survivalism to empowerment:** in which the structures that nourish the new professionalism are also, by mistake as it were, empowering schools and teachers.

These ideas offer both an example of theorising about ITE and provide some food for thought about course design. They also indicate the scope of knowledge and the breadth of vision involved in theorising about ITE.

Neither is Hargreaves alone in his attempt to make sense of the present, project into the future and derive from them new design models for ITE. Elliott also considers a new form of professional image across professions, and thus shares much in common with Schön's ideas (Schön 1987) already discussed in Chapter 2 above. He too notes the collaboration with clients in identifying, clarifying and solving their problems; the importance of communication and empathy with clients; a new emphasis on holistic understanding; 'self reflection as a means of overcoming stereotypical judgements and responses'. He concludes that the 'new professionalism' he has outlined 'has enormous implications for curriculum design in the area of professional education' (Elliott 1991, p.314). He suggests that it implies:

1.   that all professional learning that is worthwhile is experiential, including the acquisition of relevant and useful knowledge

2.   that the study of real practical situations which are problematic, complex, and open to various interpretations from various perspectives should be the core of the course

3.   that the pedagogy used to support professional learners should

aim to develop in them those capacities that are basic to competent reflective practice

4.   that acquiring knowledge should 'proceed interactively with reflecting about real practical situations'.
     (Summary of Elliott 1991, p.314)

A further set of trends that must be taken account of in considering ITE course design relates to what recent research has to teach us. In many cases (research being about theories and rarely about the discovery of empirical facts that can be extensively and usefully generalised), such literature leaves the intelligent reader with questions rather than new certainties. Kyriacou offer details of British and American research on these and other issues related to reflective practice. And Edwards comments usefully on the current nature of pedagogic theory and makes the point that research does not provide a stock of expert solutions to common classroom problems (because it is neither in the nature of research nor in that of the practical problems to be able to do so) (Edwards 1992b, p.287). There is, however, a growing body of research on student teachers as learners. Their perspectives also need to be taken account of by any theorist and course designer for ITE — especially given current trends towards giving learners more responsibility and taking more account of their views. Clark (1988) usefully reviews some work in this area and McIntyre (1988) also shows how the Oxford Internship scheme was planned on the bases of twelve areas of research, including attempts to find out more about students as learners.

Some of the tensions in ITE, then, stem from the inevitable struggle between preserving the best of past tradition and the inexorable pressures towards the new; between hard won successful practices and the unsettling of them by new *theories* derived from research knowledge. Some tensions (for example, the debate about the competence or reflective practice model) relate to the nature of the enterprise of ITE and even the nature of university education itself; some tensions relate to current conditions and future possibilities in schools and colleges; some to the current struggle to clarify exactly what can best be done by whom between teachers and tutors; and some to our developing understanding of the nature of teaching expertise, the processes of learning to teach, and an increasing understanding of the learners' perspectives. Yet further problems are raised by different views of the role of the learner and by differing views about theory and practice.

Indeed, the (healthy) lack of agreement surfaces vividly in the very lists of content areas suggested for ITE. Consider, for example, the contrast between the government's list of competences which forms the core of what ITE is considered to be about, and Shulman's seminal list of different types of teacher knowledge, all of which arguably ought to figure in an ITE course: content knowledge; general pedagogical knowledge; curriculum knowledge; knowledge of learners and their characteristics; knowledge of educational contexts; and knowledge of educational ends (Shulman 1987).

The following paragraphs offer something of the flavour of some of the more detailed arguments.

For example, there are conflicting ideas amongst teacher educators, and the overall research evidence is equally ambivalent, about the importance of transformational versus productive approaches to ITE. As a result of studying a group of undergraduates on their final teaching practice, and in contrast to the views of Skilbeck, Elliott and Hargreaves seen above, McNally *et al.* argue that they, like others before them, are 'empirically persuaded that the student teaching experience still seems to be time for receiving tradition, for learning about the professional role and having it validated by children' and that 'it may be too difficult for students to immerse themselves in the practices and cultures of teaching and to research it as well' (McNally *et al.* 1994, p.229). Yet, by comparison, Jean Rudduck aims for 'thinking teachers who will, through the quality of their work, struggle to lift the status of the profession and to improve the life chances of *all* their pupils' (Rudduck 1992, p.161).

In considering the thorny subject of the roles of tutor and teacher, college and school, Edwards, in the face of the expansion of school-centred ITT, called for a substantial academic as well as a practical base to the ITE course which recognised the gradual development of pedagogic theory. He described the contribution of HE as needing to be 'complementary and distinctive', characterised by the use of 'a wider range of contexts, curriculum developments and teaching strategies than any school can provide', involving opening up to enqiry hitherto embedded theory, and encouraging students to take an investigative, self-critical approach to their teaching 'which should draw on their tutors' own commitment to research' (Edwards 1992a, pp.288–9). Jean Rudduck, too, argues that:

> What higher education tutors can offer is an analytic perspective that is fed by observation in a range of classrooms and sharpened by the evidence of research. Our contribution is different from and complementary to that of the practising teacher.
> (Rudduck 1992, p.160)

While there are no HE voices raised against these views, there is little solid evidence of exactly how tutors do operate within the college (see Fish 1995).

This leads us into the extensive debate (most probably the central issue for ITE in the mid- to late nineties) about the role of HE and in particular 'theory' in teacher education — the rationale for its contribution to ITE, the shape in which it might contribute and the nature of that contribution.

The view that theory is 'barmy' has already been given great prominence. Smith offers one example of a response to this. He supports strongly a role for theory in ITE, reminding us of government and public views and making the point that the best antidote to 'bad theory' is 'the insistence that teachers think through ideas rigorously and in some depth'. He speculates whether there is too little theory ('rigorous, theoretical analysis') in ITE rather than too much and adds:

> For it is where there is insufficient critical, analytical thinking that the dreary orthodoxies take root and the ghosts of dead theories roam unchecked. Unless teachers have sufficient understanding of the philosophies that are *presupposed* by what is taken as evidence, the scope of their reflectivity, and thus their capacity for change, is limited from the outset, and they are condemned to remain second-class citizens in the world of ideas.
> (Smith 1992, p.391)

He also usefully suggests the term 'reflective theory' for the activities of the teacher standing back from the classroom and scrutinising what she/he is doing and examining the presuppositions and assumptions that she/he has made. He offers the term 'academic theory' for what he calls:

> a more thorough-going scrutiny in which our ideas are challenged by other people, in which we read books and test our thinking against the ideas to be found in them, where we acquire a historical perspective, [and] wrestle with quite fundamental concepts ...
> (Smith 1992, p.392)

He notes the 'near impossibility' of working at this level without the support of HE resources including staff. He makes the point that both sorts of theory are still practice-focussed (Smith 1992, pp.393). He continues: '... the question of the nature and role of educational theory, reflective and academic, is nothing less than the question of whether education is to be a properly *rational* enterprise or not'. He suggests and then explores the following key tasks for reflective and academic theory in ITE, which might be seen as students' entitlement, and which I have summarised as follows:

1. to challenge implicit theory already in students' thinking

2. to show that things can be otherwise (via history)

3. to develop a sense of education (by examining ideas, metaphors, formulating a defensible personal theory of education)

4. to create an intelligent profession (accustomed to reading thoughtful and demanding books)

5. to make education interesting (to turn the potentially confusing and internally contestable into something intrinsically interesting – and unthreatening).

If, then, these are the kinds of tensions and issues, debates and questions that the curriculum designer for ITE needs to be familiar with, what issues about curriculum design itself might be useful in this work?

Planning the course

The planners of an ITE course, then, have to seek to reduce this complexity in order to arrange the course and document it for various purposes. In this, they must, of course, conform to government requirements – including competences (until these ideas are revised), but providing these criteria are satisfied, there is no reason why the course should not also be shaped by other (perhaps more important) considerations.

Some of the complexities of planning for ITE were captured in a range of questions I have previously offered and which included the following:

● What exactly can be best learnt where?

● What are the important differences and similarities between teachers and tutors?

● What kinds of assessment will help students learn to teach? (See Fish 1989, pp.96–8)

Stenhouse's important curriculum design models – the product, process and research models (Stenhouse 1975) were also reviewed in that book. And examples of courses that are currently in operation at Oxford, Cambridge and Exeter have been described above. The mentor wishing to contribute to course planning might find it useful to be aware of these.

One further important framework is offered by Grundy (1987) (see also above, pp.181), who, by harnessing Habermas's ideas and relating them to the work of Stenhouse, provides a three-fold definition of curriculum as technique, practice and praxis. Curriculum as technique is rooted in the TR view of teaching as described in Chapter 2 above, and would be structured by the product-centred approach to curriculum design sometimes known as 'the objectives model' (see Stenhouse 1975, pp.52–83). Here, knowledge is given and controlled in a hierarchical setting and success is judged entirely in terms of outcomes.

By contrast, curriculum as practice is expressed in curriculum design terms by Stenhouse's process model (Stenhouse 1975, pp.84–96). It is concerned with understanding in its widest sense – particularly understanding the environment in order to interact responsibly with it. This involves the production of knowledge by making meaning and demands a consensual approach to interpretation of knowledge. Success here is judged in terms of whether the 'interpreted meaning assisted the process of making judgements about how to act rationally and morally' (Grundy 1987, p.14).

The third definition sees curriculum in emancipatory terms. This emerges for Habermas from a critique of both previous approaches. The technical approach fails to facilitate autonomy and responsibility since it has an interest in control. The practical approach comes closer to serving the interests of autonomy and responsibility but (though it has potential for freedom through its emphasis on consensual meaning) it is 'inadequate for the promotion of true emancipation precisely because of the propensity of persons to be deceived, even when understandings are arrived at in open discussion and debate'. The emancipatory approach, therefore, is concerned with freeing persons from the 'coercion of the technical and the possible deceit of the practical' (see Grundy 1987, p.17). The approach is concerned therefore 'with *empowerment*, that is, the ability of individuals and groups to take control of their own lives in autonomous and responsible ways'. This is achieved by means of gaining authentic critical insight via the social construction of meaning. In practice it 'will involve the participants [both teacher and pupil] in the educational encounter, ... which attempts to change the structures within which learning occurs and which constrain freedom in often un-recognized ways' (Grundy 1993, p.19).

What overall intention, then, should shape the ITE curriculum? There is much here to be debated. Given the critique of the technical approach offered above, but the government demands for competences at the heart of the course, how can this approach be accommodated in a more educational design? Can ways be found of breaking out of the technical mould? How will ITE in Britain relate to its counterpart in Europe if the essentially reproductive nature of teaching and learning at the heart of the technical approach is allowed to prevent it from evolving? Where can space be found in the ITE programme to air these very issues? How can time be found for the partners to discuss them?

Meanwhile, current courses have to be run, and the details of the school-based programme have to be decided and its quality assurance arrangements have to be clear too. It is to this that we must now turn.

(ii)

The school programme and quality assurance

Unless it is merely a skills training of the kind eschewed above, the school-based programme must be properly set within the course as a whole and cannot be established before course aims, rationale and structure have been decided. When it is established, it needs to consider the class-based work and the whole-school work as an entity, and to indicate clearly how it articulates with the rest of the course, how tutors and mentors relate and what the quality assurance procedures will consist of. This brief section offers some principles for school-based work, some practical considerations relating to its planning and operation and refers the reader to some examples of such programmes. It ends with some comments on quality assurance at school level.

Wilkin, in an article which draws on a consideration of both the Oxford and the Cambridge pioneering courses, offers some important basic course design principles. She makes the points that the work in school should be well structured, justifiable and articulated, with clearly documented and agreed responsibilities for the school which have been negotiated between the partners, so that the content and ownership of each area is well defined. In this, the school and the HE involvement 'should be regarded as of equal worth with respect to their contribution to training' since they represent the various areas of knowledge that the student needs to draw upon, and are thus indispensable. She adds that the training programme should demonstrate continuity and development, so that the student can make use of and build upon earlier experiences (see Wilkin 1992b, p.87). Above all she declares that the content and form of the school programme 'should be justified by reference to principles' and should indicate why the school has taken on certain responsibilities and why the training programme has been structured as it has. This programme should be available to everyone and should state clearly the procedures for assessment of the student, the accountability of the mentor, the evaluation of the course and the assurance of quality (Wilkin 1992b, p.87–8).

These very useful starting points have been supplemented by the work of McIntyre, Haggar and Burn (1994). They offer those designing a school-based programme some useful principles, as follows: **progression; responsiveness; negotiation; depth and breadth; coherence;** and **making the most of different approaches** (see McIntyre, Haggar and Burn 1994, pp.50–3 for the details). They also make the point that each school needs its own programme and that this is best worked out between a school-attached tutor who knows the whole course and the school team. (This is fairly normal practice and has usually grown out of earlier partnership arrangements in many HEIs.) In a very useful and extensive chapter they consider details about timetabling of this work and the practical arrangements with the HEI, teaching methods and alternative ways of shaping the programme (see McIntyre, Haggar and Burn 1994, pp.47–83).

Matters related to the quality assurance dimension of the school-based programme are referred to briefly by Wilkin who makes the point that mentors, like tutors, will have to demonstrate accountability and that this 'may include demonstrating that they are fit persons to undertake responsible and continuous student training, that they have planned their training work systematically and with an understanding of student needs, that they are keeping adequate records of student performance' (Wilkin 1992b, p.89). But these matters are not easy to systematise into a quality assurance system across all the schools involved in school-based training. Even two years later McIntyre, Haggar and Burn indicate that 'many universities and colleges are still working at establishing adequate quality assurance procedures' (McIntyre, Haggar and Burn 1994, p.41).

But it is of course possible to make some simple suggestions. For example, the need for a *range* of mentors necessary for any school to attend to the different aspects of students' requirements on placement, indicates the need for a system with clear structures, known to students and staff, documented and evaluated. This is particularly so since mentors will be both assessing students as well as working alongside them. Indeed, there may need to be a co-ordinator within the school and also, given the number of schools in partnership, perhaps a committee across schools. Certainly the instructions to inspectors for ITT state that such matters are vital. Good or very good gradings are to be given, according to one handbook, only to schools: with regular, planned meetings between staff and students which focus on educational issues; where there are clearly planned opportunities for students' involvement in the life of the school (staff meetings, parents' evenings, curricular activities); where timetable provision is well organised and clearly documented and supported by an appropriate assessment system; where a variety of effective teaching approaches, based on clear learning targets, are demonstrated; where there are arrangements for staff to share their assessment of students and evaluate the experience of training; where there are arrangements for staff to share in student evaluation with other partners in ITE; where students are involved in the identification of their own assessment; where there is a systematic programme of good quality for developing competences and regular meetings of staff to plan and evaluate; and where there is effective monitoring of students against competences and a stimulus to self-evaluation and critical thinking by students. These matters, however, are perhaps best regarded by those just beginning this work, as targets for the mid-term.

Indeed, as Taylor emphasises, none of these structures and inspectorial approaches is as important as what he calls 'designed-in quality', by which he means, it is the quality of what students see, hear, read, write, think about, say and perform that determines the effectiveness of teacher education (Taylor 1994, p.171). He also emphasises that it is the processes of critique and negotiation, of selection and pondering alternatives that affect quality, not the documents, the validation procedures and the audits. Quality, he says, can happen only if the right people are chosen to educate and induct teachers, and so systematic staff development is a vital component, together with 'a collaborative structure for designing, scrutinizing, approving, and reviewing the content and pedagogy of teacher education' (see Taylor 1994, p.173).

And this leads naturally to the last (and what might equally have been the very first) issue in quality mentoring – the quality of the mentor – and the impact on the school of quality mentoring.

(iii)

Quality mentoring and the school

The HEIs have been left to determine the quality indicators that they would seek from a school to determine whether they would invite them into partnership. Of course the obvious contenders are: a good OFSTED report; ITE written in as a priority to the school's development plan; the school ethos being conducive to reflection on practice; clear evidence that staff engage in reflection and investigation of practice; evidence that the school is an open institution; evidence that staff are able to articulate the principles beneath their practice; and evidence of readiness *as a school* to work with ITE students – which means everyone seeing this in a positive light. This may be a scene that exists where the head of the school is already a shining light in this respect (see, for example, Shaw 1992). But more realistically, ITE is likely to be one of many pressing issues for a school and to be dependent on some few who, though keenly committed, are less influential than the head. Such staff, whose experience will have developed as a result of work in earlier (individual) partnerships with HEIs, will now need to drive staff development in a school gradually in the direction of a whole-school view and then a whole-school policy in action. (And this is likely to be the case notwithstanding the proliferation of short mentoring courses being mounted by HEIs in the mid-1990s.)

Thus, the indicators listed above may be more likely to become a mark of having been involved long-term with ITE under the new arrangements rather than an indicator of readiness to begin. This section, therefore, in the spirit of the rest of this book, offers some brief frameworks that might help the lone mentor with ambition to improve self and influence school. For schools that wish to involve themselves in major whole-school programmes there are already distance learning packs (see Haggar, Burn and McIntyre 1993; Rowie Shaw 1992 – especially Appendix 3, which offers a model whole school policy on ITE; and Watkins and Whalley 1993).

The quality mentor: an overview

TASK 9.1: POINTS FOR CONSIDERATION

1. Reconsider the agenda you made at the start of the book, and check whether you have achieved what you intended to.

2. Review the main areas of your learning and trace your changing ideas. What has caused you to make these changes?

3. Jot down the key characteristics of a mentor that make for quality mentoring.

4. Compare your list with the list below.

What attributes are involved in being a quality mentor? Like all educational questions the answers will be value-based. Readers might like to consider the main values underlying the following list.

- being a learner and a seeker and willing to tackle new ideas and practices

- being willing to open up practice and knowing how, when and to what end to do this with students so that they can think critically about theirs

- being able to offer constructive debriefing which will lead ultimately to student self-assessment

- being able to demonstrate a variety of teaching strategies, to talk about even more, and to cope with the unexpected

- being able to demonstrate that one's practice is principled

- being able to enunciate some of those principles

- being willing to open up to discussion one's ideas

- being aware of the value-base of one's work

- being able to pin-point and explain the underlying theories of one's practice

- being someone who reflects on practice and is self-critical

- being someone who investigates practice with a view to refining it

- understanding the problematic nature of issues

- being able to cope with ideological conflicts and educational debates

- being able to lead students to reflective theorising

- knowing what one is and isn't sure of, and saying so openly

- being tolerant, open-minded and able to live with one's uncertainties

- being happy to enable others to find their own ways (with one's own class!)

- being able to cope with both the role of enabler and the role of assessor

- being aware of the moral dimension to teaching

- knowing about the wider dimensions of ITE and being able to see it holistically

- being a reader of professional literature

- knowing about and keeping up with government requirements of ITE (circulars and parliamentary acts)

- being flexible and able to cope with the wide range of role demanded in mentoring (interviewing, curriculum planning, lecturing, teaching, investigating, reflecting, counselling).

In short, perhaps, these might be summarised as having suitable personal qualities and taking a principled approach to practice. And this leaves us with the final question: What sort of impact might this whole approach to mentoring have on the whole school?

The impact of mentoring on the school

The physical and mental demands on a school of involvement in ITE under the new arrangements cannot be denied. It affects the organisation and management, the daily working conditions of staff, the pupils, the ethos of the school and the general atmosphere. And in this, wheels will need to be oiled, feathers smoothed and even dignity reinstated. (Long-experienced ITE tutors who have carried many an oil-can may even smile at the thought that such activities now fall to the professional tutor *within* the school.)

But any local difficulties ought to be far outweighed by the extensive benefits. Put in a nutshell, the activity of mentoring for ITE and of seeking to become a quality mentor is a major staff development activity. If it has not already begun, the time to begin it is now. One possible beginning might be to start by staff simply sharing the experiences of reflection on and investigation of their own practice and experimenting in explaining to each other the principles underlying their practice, their espoused theories and their theories-in-use. (Some of the tasks offered in early chapters above might be helpful here, and see also McIntyre (1994).) Then, assuming that any member of a school staff who works in any way with a student is a mentor, one approach to looking at involvement of the whole school is to discuss:

- some attributes involved in being an ITE mentor (see above for examples)

- what knowledge is involved in being an ITE mentor?

- what, in the ethos of the school, provides for these things? (What enables – or would enable – the school to become a more reflective community?)

- what expertise is already available where?

- what staff development provision is now needed?

Such questions lead on to considering whether the school is a learning school, and a reflective school. And these lead on to the quest for improving schooling through professional development (see especially Osterman and Kottkamp (1993, Chapter 3) which looks in detail at nurturing reflection in the school). There is always more to do and more to learn. Quality in education is not achieved by decree but by the endless pursuit of greater understanding and better practice.

If this work is demanding, we must surely not complain. To work with student teachers is to prepare for the education of children yet unborn. We cannot give of less than our best when the future of the twenty-first century is in our hands.

Further reading

Fish, D. (1989) *Learning through practice in initial teacher training*. London: Kogan Page. (See especially Chapter 6.)

Fish, D. (Ed.) (1995) *Quality learning for student teachers: university tutors' educational practices*. London: David Fulton.

Edwards, T. (1992) 'Issues and challenges in initial teacher education', *Cambridge Journal of Education*, **22** (3), pp.283–92.

Elliott, J. (1991) 'A model of professionalism and its implications for teacher education', *British Education Research Journal*, **17** (4), pp.309–18.

McIntyre, D. (1994) 'Classrooms as learning environments for beginning teachers', in Wilkin, M. and Sankey, D. (Eds) (1994) *Collaboration and transition in initial teacher training*. London: Kogan Page.

McIntyre, D., Haggar, H. and Burn, K. (1994) *The management of student teachers' learning*. London: Kogan Page.

Osterman, K. and Kottkamp, R. (1993) *Reflective practice for educators: improving schooling through professional development*. California: Corwin Press Inc.

Shaw, R. (1992) *Teacher training in the secondary school*. London: Kogan Page.

Smith, R. (1992) 'Theory: an entitlement to understanding', *Cambridge Journal of Education*, **22** (3), pp.387–98.

References

Alexander, R. (1990) 'Partnership in initial teacher education: confronting the issues', in Booth, M., Furlong, J. and Wilkin, M. (Eds) (1990) *Partnership in initial teacher training*. London: Cassell, pp.59–73.

Anning, A., Broadhead, P., Busher, H., Clarke, S., Dodgson, H., Taggart, L., White, S. and Wilson, R. (1990) *Using video-recordings for teacher professional development*. Leeds: University of Leeds.

Argyris, C. and Schön, D.A. (1974) *Theory in practice*. San Francisco: Jossey Bass.

Ashworth, P.D. and Saxton, J. (1990) 'On competence', *Journal of Further and Higher Education*, **14** (2), pp.3–25.

Barber, M. (1993) 'Till death do us part', *Times Educational Supplement* (28.5.93), p.16.

Barrett, E., Barton, L., Furlong, J., Galvin, C., Miles, S. and Whitty, G. (1992) *Initial teacher education in England and Wales: a topography* (Modes of Teacher Education Research Project). London: Goldsmiths College.

Bekhradnia, B. (1994) 'Buffer body with good track record', *Times Higher Educational Supplement* (27.5.94), p.13.

Benner, P. (1984) *From novice to expert*. California: Wesley Addison.

Bennett, N. and Carré, C. (Eds) (1993) *Learning to teach*. London: Routledge.

Bernbaum, G., Patrick, H. and Reid, K. (1985) 'A history of post-graduate initial teacher education in England and Wales, 1880–1980', in Hopkins, D. and Reid, K. (Eds) (1985) *Rethinking teacher education*. London: Croom Helm, pp.7–18.

Berrill, M. (1992) 'Structured mentoring and the development of teaching skill', in Wilkin, M. (Ed.) (1992a) *Mentoring in schools*. London: Kogan Page, pp.155–72.

Booth, M., Furlong, J. and Wilkin, M. (Eds) (1990) *Partnership in initial teacher training*. London: Cassell.

Boud, D., Keogh, R. and Walker, D. (Eds) (1985) *Reflection: turning experience into learning*. London: Kogan Page.

Bridges, D., Elliott, J. and Klass, C. (1986) 'Performance appraisal as naturalistic enquiry: a report of the fourth Cambridge conference on educational evaluation', *Cambridge Journal of Education,* **16** (3), pp.221–33.

Broadfoot, P. (Ed.) (1986) *Profiles and records of achievement: a review of issues and practice*. Eastbourne: Holt Education.

Broadhead, P. (1987) 'A blue-print for the good teacher? The HMI/DES model of good primary practice', *British Journal of Educational Studies*, **35** (1), pp.57–71.

Broadhead, P. (1990a) 'Filming and reflecting on primary practice: partnerships explored', in Anning, A. *et al.* (1990) *Using video-recordings for teacher professional development*. Leeds: University of Leeds, pp.20–36.

Broadhead, P. (1990b) 'Perceptual issues in the use of video in educational research', in Anning, A. *et al.* (1990) *Using video-recordings for teacher professional development*. Leeds: University of Leeds, pp.124–39.

Brown, S. and McIntyre, D. (1993) *Making sense of teaching*. Buckingham: Open University Press.

Bullough, R. and Gitlin, A. (1994) 'Challenging teacher education as training: four propositions', *Journal of Education for Teaching*, **20** (1), pp.67–82.

Burgess, R. (1985) *Field methods in the study of education*. London: Falmer Press.

Burke, J. (Ed.) (1989) *Competency-based education and training*. London: Falmer Press.

Burn, K. (1992) 'Collaborative teaching', in Wilkin, M. (Ed.) (1992a) *Mentoring in schools*. London: Kogan Page, pp.133–43.

Calderhead, J. (Ed.) (1988) *Teachers' professional learning*. London: Falmer Press.

Calderhead, J. (1989) 'Reflective teaching and teacher education', *Teaching and Teacher Education*, **5** (1), pp.43–51.

Calderhead, J. and Gates, P. (Eds) (1993) *Conceptualising reflection in teacher development*. London: Falmer Press.

Cameron-Jones, M. (1991) *Training teachers: a practical guide*. Edinburgh: Scottish Council for Research in Education.

Carr, D. (1992) 'Four dimensions of educational professionalism', *Westminster Studies in Education*, **15** (1), pp.19–33.

Carr, D. (1993) 'Questions of competence', *British Journal of Educational Studies*, **41** (3), pp.253–71.

Carr, W. (1987) 'What is an educational practice?', *Journal of Philosophy of Education*, **21** (2), pp.163–75.

Carr, W. (Ed.) (1989) *Quality in teaching: arguments for a reflective profession*. London: Falmer Press.

Carr, W. and Kemmis, S. (1986) *Becoming critical: education, knowledge and action research*. London: Falmer Press.

CATE (1986) *Catenote 4: links between initial training institutions and schools*. London: CATE.

CATE (1992) *The accreditation of initial teacher training under Circular 9/92*. London: CATE.

CATE (1993) *The initial training of primary school teachers: Circular 14/93 (England): A note of guidance*. London: CATE.

Chown, A. and Last, J. (1993) 'Can the NCVQ model be used for teacher training?' *Journal of Further and Higher Education*, **17** (2), pp.15–26.

Clark, C.M. (1988) 'Asking the right questions about teacher preparation: contributions of research on teacher thinking', *Educational Researcher*, **17** (1), pp.5–12.

CNAA (1991) *Placement training: the primary placement project (Briefing Paper No. 26)*. London: CNAA.

CNAA (1992a) *Competence-based approaches to teacher education: viewpoints and issues*. London: CNAA.

CNAA (1992b) *Profiling in higher education: guidelines for the development and use of profiling schemes*. London: CNAA.

CNAA (1992c) *Continuity between initial training and induction in teacher education: sharing roles in assessing professional practice*. London: CNAA.

Davies, I. (1993) 'Using profiling in initial teacher education', *Journal of Further and Higher Education*, **17** (2), pp.227–39.

DES (1978) *Primary education in England*. London: HMSO.

DES (1979) *Aspects of secondary education*. London: HMSO.

DES (1983) *Teaching in schools: the content of initial training*. London: HMSO.

DES (1984) *Initial teacher training: approval of courses (Circular 3/84)*. London: DES.

DES (1987) *School teachers' pay and conditions*. London: HMSO.

DES (1988) *Qualified teacher status: a consultation document*. London: HMSO.

DES (1989) *Initial teacher training: approval of courses (Circular 24/89)*. London: DES.

DFE (1992) *Initial teacher training (secondary phase) (Circular 9/92)*. London: DFE.

DFE (1993) *The initial training of primary school teachers: new criteria for courses (Circular 14/93)*. London: DFE.

Dewey, J. (1933) *How we think*. Boston: D.C. Heath & Co.

Diamond, C.T.P. (1991) *Teacher education as transformation*. Milton Keynes: Open University.

Dreyfus, H.L. and Dreyfus, S.E. (1986) *Mind over machine*. New York: Free Press.

Dunne, E. and Dunne, R. (1993) 'The purpose and impact of school-based work: the class-teacher's role', in Bennett, N. and Carré, C. (Eds) (1993) *Learning to teach*. London: Routledge, pp.135–48.

Dunne, R. and Harvard, G. (1993) 'A model of teaching and its implications for mentoring', in McIntyre, D., Haggar, H. and Wilkin, M. (Eds) (1993) *Mentoring: perspectives on school-based teacher education*. London: Kogan Page, pp.117–29.

Edwards, T. (1992a) *Change and reform in initial teacher education (Briefing No. 9)*. London: National Commission for Education.

Edwards, T. (1992b) 'Issues and challenges in initial teacher education', *Cambridge Journal of Education*, **22** (3), pp.283–91.

Edwards, T. (1994) 'The Universities Council for the Education and Training of Teachers: defending an interest or fighting a cause?' *Journal of Education for Teaching*, **20** (2), pp.143–52.

Elliott, J. (1989) 'Appraisal of performance or appraisal of persons', in Simons, H. and Elliott, J. (Eds) (1989) *Rethinking appraisal and assessment*. Milton Keynes: Open University Press, pp.80–99.

Elliott, J. (1991) 'A model of professionalism and its implications for teacher education', *British Education Research Journal*, **17** (4), pp.309–18.

Eraut, M. (1989) 'Initial teacher training and the NVQ model', in Burke, J. (Ed.) (1989) *Competency-based education and training*. London: Falmer Press, pp.171–85.

Fish, D. (1989) *Learning through practice in initial teacher training*. London: Kogan Page.

Fish, D. (Ed.) (1995) *Quality learning for student teachers: university tutors' educational practices*. London: David Fulton.

Fish, D. and Purr, B. (1991) *An evaluation of practice-based learning in continuing education in nursing, midwifery and health visiting*. London: The English National Board for Nursing, Midwifery and Health Visiting.

Fish, D., Twinn, S. and Purr, B. (1990) *How to enable learning through professional practice*. London: West London Press.

Fish, D., Twinn, S. and Purr, B. (1991) *Promoting reflection: improving the supervision of practice in health visiting and initial teacher training*. London: West London Institute.

Gardner, P. (1993) 'The early history of school-based teacher training', in McIntyre, D., Haggar, H. and Wilkin, M. (Eds) (1993) *Mentoring: perspectives on school-based teacher education*. London: Kogan Page, pp.21–36.

Garland, P. (1994) 'Using competence-based assessment positively on Certificate in Education programmes', *Journal of Further and Higher Education*, **18** (2), pp.16–22.

Gilroy, P. (1993) 'Reflections on Schön: an epistemological critique and a practical alternative', in Gilroy, P. and Smith, M. (Eds) (1993) *International Analysis of Teacher Education: Journal of Education for Teaching*, **19** (4/5), pp.125–42.

Golby, M. (1981) 'Practice and theory', in Lawn, M. and Barton, L. (Eds) (1981) *Rethinking curriculum studies*. London: Croom Helm, pp.214–36.

Golby, M. (1989) 'Teachers and their research', in Carr, W. (Ed.) (1989) *Quality in teaching*. London: Falmer Press, pp.163–72.

Golby, M. (1993a) 'Editorial comments' in a reader provided for M.Ed. students at Exeter University (limited publication). Tiverton: Fair Way Publications.

Golby, M. (1993b) 'Mentorship a professional model' (unpublished paper), University of Exeter.

Golby, M. (1993c) *Case study as educational research*. Tiverton: Fair Way Publications.

Goldhammer, R. (1969) *Clinical supervision*. New York: Holt Rinehart and Winston.

Goodyear, R. (1992) 'The inservice curriculum for teachers: a review of policy, control and balance', *British Journal of Educational Studies*, **40** (4), pp.379–99.

Gore, J.M. (1991) 'Practising what we preach: action research into the supervision of student teachers', in Tabachnick, R. and Zeichner, K. (Eds) (1991) *Issues and practices in inquiry-oriented teacher education*. London: Falmer Press, pp.253–72.

Grace, G. (1985) 'Judging teachers: the social and political contexts of teacher education', *British Journal of the Sociology of Education*, **6** (1), pp.3–15.

Griffiths, M. and Tann, S. (1992) 'Using reflective practice to link personal and public theories', *Journal of Education for Teaching*, **18** (1), pp.69–84.

Grundy, S. (1987) *Curriculum: product or praxis?* London: Falmer Press.

Haggar, H., Burn, K. and McIntyre, D. (1993) *The school mentor handbook*. London: Kogan Page.

Hansen, D. (1993) 'The moral importance of the teacher's style', *Journal of Curriculum Studies*, **25** (5), pp.397–421.

Hargreaves, D. (1994) 'The new professionalism: the synthesis of professional and institutional development', *Teaching and Teacher Education*, **10** (4), 423–38.

Hartley, D. (1992) *Teacher appraisal: a policy analysis*. Edinburgh: Scottish Academic Press.

Hartley, D. (1993) 'Confusion in teacher education: a post-modern condition', in Gilroy, P. and Smith, M. (Eds) (1993) *International Analysis of Teacher Education: Journal of Education for Teaching*, **19** (4/5), pp.83–9.

Harvard, G. and Dunne, R. (1992) 'The role of the mentor in developing teacher competence', *Westminster Studies in Education*, **15** (1), pp.33–44.

Hatton, E. (1985) 'Team teaching and teaching orientation to work: implications for the pre-service and inservice preparation of teachers', *Journal of Education for Teaching*, **11** (3), pp.228–44.

Hitchcock, G. (1989) *Profiles and profiling: a practical introduction*. Harlow: Longman.

HMI (1991) *School-based initial teacher training in England and Wales*. London: HMSO.

HMSO (1993) *The government's proposals for the reform of initial teacher training*. London: HMSO.

Holly, M.L. (1984) *Keeping a personal-professional journal*. Geelong: Deakin University.

Holly, M.L. (1989) 'Perspectives on teacher appraisal and professional development', in Simons, H. and Elliott, J. (Eds) (1989) *Rethinking appraisal and assessment*. Milton Keynes: Open University Press, pp.100–18.

Hopkins, D. (1985) *A teacher's guide to classroom research*. Milton Keynes: Open University Press.

Hopkins, D. and Reid, K. (Eds) (1985) *Rethinking teacher education*. London: Croom Helm.

Hoyle, E. (1974) 'Professionality, professionalism and the control of teaching', *London Educational Review*, **3** (2), pp.13–18.

James, M. (1989) 'Negotiation and dialogue in student assessment and teacher appraisal', in Simons, H. and Elliott, J. (Eds) (1989)

Rethinking appraisal and assessment. Milton Keynes: Open University Press, pp.149–60.

Jarvis, P. (1994) 'Learning practical knowledge', *Journal of Further and Higher Education*, **18** (1), pp.31–43.

Johnson, S. (1994) 'Is action research a natural process for teachers?', *Educational Action Research: An International Journal*, **2** (1), pp.38–49.

Kenny, W.W. and Grotelleuschen, A. (1984) 'Making the case for case study', *Journal of Curriculum Studies*, **16** (1), pp.37–51.

Kolb, D. (1984) *Experiential learning: experience as the source of learning and development*. New Jersey: Prentice Hall.

Kydd, L. and Weir, D. (1993) 'Initial teacher training: the professional route to technician status', *British Journal of Educational Studies*, **41** (3), pp.400–11.

Kyriacou, C. (1993) 'Research on the development of expertise in classroom teaching during initial teacher training and the first year of teaching', *Educational Review*, **45** (1), pp.78–88.

Langford, G. (1978) *Teaching as a profession: an essay in the philosophy of education*. London: Macmillan.

Law, H. (1984) *The uses and abuses of profiling*. London: Harper and Row.

Lucas, P. (1991) 'Reflection, new practices, and the need for flexibility in supervising student teachers', *Journal of Further and Higher Education*, **15** (2), pp.84–93.

McIntyre, D. (1988) 'Designing a teacher education curriculum from research and theory on teacher knowledge', in Calderhead, J. (Ed.) (1988) *Teachers' Professional Learning*. London: Falmer Press, pp.97–114.

McIntyre, D. (1989) 'Criterion-referenced assessment of teaching', in Simons, H. and Elliott, J. (Eds) (1989) *Rethinking appraisal and assessment*. Milton Keynes: Open University Press, pp.64–71.

McIntyre, D. (1990) 'The Oxford internship scheme and the Cambridge analytical framework: models of partnership in initial teacher education', in Booth, M., Furlong, J. and Wilkin, M. (1990) *Partnership in initial teacher training*. London: Cassell, pp.110–27.

McIntyre, D. (1993) 'Theory, theorizing and reflection in initial teacher education', in Calderhead, J. and Gates, P. (Eds) (1993) *Conceptualising reflection in teacher education*. London: Falmer Press, pp.39–52.

McIntyre, D. (1994) 'Classrooms as learning environments for beginning teachers', in Wilkin, M. and Sankey, D. (Eds) (1994) *Collaboration and transition in initial teacher training*. London: Kogan Page, pp.81–93.

McIntyre, D., Haggar, H. and Burn, K. (1993) *Mentoring: perspectives on school-based teacher education*. London: Kogan Page.

McIntyre, D. and Haggar, H. (1993) 'Teachers' expertise and models of mentoring', in McIntyre, D., Haggar, H. and Wilkin, M. (Eds) (1993) *Mentoring: perspectives on school-based teacher education*. London: Kogan Page, pp.86–102.

McIntyre, D., Haggar, H. and Burn, K. (1994) *The management of student teachers' learning*. London: Kogan Page.

McLaughlin, T.H. (1994) 'Mentoring and the demands of reflection', in Wilkin, M. and Sankey, D. (Eds) (1994) *Collaboration and transition* in initial teacher training. London: Kogan Page, pp.151–60.

McNally, J., Cope, P., Inglis, B. and Stronach, I. (1994) 'Current realities in the student teaching experience: a preliminary enquiry', *Teaching and Teacher Education*, **10** (2), pp.219–30.

Mansfield, B. (1989) 'Competence and standards', in Burke, J. (Ed.) (1989) *Competency-based education and training*. London: Falmer Press, pp.26–38.

Maynard, T. and Furlong, J. (1993) 'Learning to teach and models of mentoring', in McIntyre, D., Haggar, H. and Wilkin, M. (Eds) (1993) *Mentoring: perspectives on school-based teacher education*. London: Kogan Page, pp.69–85.

Mercer, D. and Abbott, I. (1989) 'Democratic learning in teacher education: partnership supervision in the teaching practice', *Journal of Education for Teaching*, **15** (2), pp.141–8.

Mitchell, L. (1989) 'The definition of standards and their assessment', in Burke, J. (Ed.) (1989) *Competency-based education and training*. London: Falmer Press, pp.54–64.

Nance, D. and Fawns, R. (1994) 'Teachers' working knowledge and training: the Australian agenda for the reform of teacher education', *Journal of Education for Teaching*, **19** (2), pp.159–74.

NCC (1991) *The National Curriculum and the initial training of student, articled and licensed teachers*. London: NCC.

Nias, J. (1987) *Seeing anew: teachers' theories of action*. Geelong: Deakin University.

OFSTED (1993a) *The training of primary school teachers, March 1991 to March 1992*. London: HMSO.

OFSTED (1993b) *The licensed teacher scheme, September 1990 to July 1992*. London: HMSO.

OFSTED (1993c) *The articled teacher scheme, September 1990 to July 1992*. London: HMSO.

OFSTED (1993d) *Well-managed classes in primary schools: case studies of six teachers*. London: OFSTED.

Osterman, K. and Kottcamp, R. (1993) *Reflective practice for educators: improving schooling through professional development*. California: Corwin Press Inc.

Passmore, J. 1980, *The philosophy of teaching*. London: Duckworth Press.

Pinar, W. (1986) '"Whole, bright and deep with understanding": issues in qualitative research and autobiographical method', in Taylor, P. (Ed.) (1986) *Recent developments in curriculum studies*. Windsor: NFER/Nelson, pp.3–18.

Pollard, A. and Tann, S. (1987) *Reflective teaching in the primary school*. London: Cassell.

Price, C. (1994) 'A new *vice anglaise*', *Times Educational Supplement* (14.1.94), p.19.

Pring, R. (1994) 'The year 2000', in Wilkin M. and Sankey, D. (Eds) (1994) *Collaboration and transition in initial teacher training*. London: Kogan Page, pp.178–89.

Reid, K. (1985) 'Recent research and developments in teacher education in England and Wales', in Hopkins, D. and Reid, K. (Eds) (1985) *Rethinking teacher education*. London: Croom Helm, pp.19–37.

Reid, W. (1979) *Thinking about the curriculum: the nature and treatment of curriculum problems*. London: Routledge and Kegan Paul.

Rudduck, J. (1992) 'Practitioner research and programmes of initial teacher education', in Russell, T. and Munby, H. (Eds) (1992) *Teachers and Teaching: from classrooms to reflection*. London: Falmer Press, pp.156–70.

Rudduck, J. and Hopkins, D. (Eds) (1985) *Research as a basis for teaching: readings from the work of Lawrence Stenhouse*. London: Heinemann.

Rudduck, J. and Sigsworth, A. (1985) 'Partnership supervision: or Goldhammer revisited', in Hopkins, D. and Reid, K. (Eds) (1985) *Rethinking teacher education*. London: Croom Helm, pp.153–71.

Russell, T. (1989) 'Documenting reflection-in-action in the classroom: searching for appropriate methods', *Qualitative Studies in Education*, **2** (4), pp.277–84.

Russell, T. (1993a) 'Teachers' professional knowledge and the future of teacher education', in Gilroy, P. and Smith, M. (Eds) (1993) *International Analysis of Teacher Education, Journal of Teacher Education*, **19** (4/5), pp.205–15.

Russell, T. (1993b), 'Critical attributes of a reflective teacher: is agreement possible?', in Calderhead, J. and Gates, P. (Eds) (1993) *Conceptualising reflection in teacher development*. London: Falmer Press, pp.144–53.

Russell, T. and Munby, H. (1991) 'Reframing: the role of experience in developing teachers' professional knowledge', in Schön D. (Ed.) (1991) *The reflective turn: case studies in and on educational practice*. New York: College Teachers Press, pp.164–87.

Russell, T. and Munby, H. (Eds) (1993) *Teachers and teaching: from classroom to reflection*. London: Falmer Press.

Schön, D.A. (1983) *The reflective practitioner*. New York: Basic Books.

Schön, D.A. (1987) *Educating the reflective practitioner*. London: Jossey Bass.

Schön, D.A. (Ed.) (1991) *The reflective turn: case studies in and on educational practice*. New York: Teachers College Press.

Schwab, J. (1969) 'The practical: a language for the curriculum', *School Review* (November), pp.1–23.

Shaw, R. (1992) *Teacher training in the secondary school*. London: Kogan Page.

Shulman, L.S. (1987) 'Knowledge and teaching: foundations of the new reform', *Harvard Educational Review*, **57** (1), pp.1–22.

Skilbeck, M. (1992) 'The role of research in teacher education', *European Journal of Teacher Education*, **15** (1/2), pp.23–31.

Smith, R. (1992) 'Theory: an entitlement to understanding', *Cambridge Journal of Education*, **22** (3), pp.387–98.

Smith, R. and Alred, G. (1993) 'The impersonation of wisdom', in McIntyre, D., Haggar, H. and Wilkin, M. (Eds) (1993) *Mentoring: perspectives on school-based teacher education*. London: Kogan Page, pp.103–16.

Smyth, J. (Ed.) (1986) *Learning about teaching through clinical supervision*. London: Croom Helm.

Squirrell, G., Gilroy, P., Jones, D. and Rudduck, J. (1990), *Acquiring* knowledge in initial teacher education. (Library and Information Research Report No. 79). London: The British Library.

Stengelhofen, J. (1993) *Teaching students in clinical settings*. London: Chapman and Hall.

Stenhouse, L. (1975) *An introduction to curriculum research and development*. London: Heinemann.

Stones, E. (1983) 'Never mind the quality: feel the ideology', editorial in *Journal of Education for Teaching*, **9** (3), pp.207−9.

Stones, E. (1992a) 'Under what influences?', *Journal of Education for Teaching*, **18** (3), pp.219−20.

Stones, E. (1992b) *Quality teaching: a sample of cases*. London: Routledge.

Stronach, I. (1989) 'A critique of the "new assessment": from currency to carnival?', in Simons, H. and Elliott, J. (Eds) (1989) *Rethinking appraisal and assessment*. Milton Keynes: Open University Press, pp.161−79.

Tabachnick, R. and Zeichner, K. (Eds) (1991) *Issues and practices in inquiry-oriented teacher education*. London: Falmer Press.

Taylor, W. (1994) 'Quality assurance', in Wilkin, M. and Sankey, D. (Eds) (1994) *Collaboration and transition in initial teacher training*. London: Kogan Page, pp.161−73.

Tripp, D. (1993) *Critical incidents in teaching: developing professional judgement*. London: Routledge.

Tuxworth, E. (1989) 'Competence based education and training: background and origins', in Burke, J. (Ed.) (1989) *Competency-based education and training*. London: Falmer Press, pp.10−25.

Van Manen, M. (1990) 'Beyond assumptions: shifting the limits of action research', *Theory into Practice*, **30** (3), pp.152−57.

Vaughan, G. (1992) 'Profiling: a mechanism for the professional development of students', *Cambridge Journal of Education*, **22** (2), pp.163−75.

Walker, R. (1985) *Doing classroom research: a handbook for teachers*. London: Methuen.

Walker, R. (1986) 'The conduct of educational case studies: ethics, theory and procedures', in Hammersley, M. (Ed.) (1986) *Controversies in classroom research*. Milton Keynes: Open University Press, pp.187−219.

Ward, D. and Richie, R. (1994) 'Profiling in initial teacher education to support professional development in primary science', *Teacher Development*, **3** (2), pp.105−19.

Watkins, C. (1992) 'An experiment in mentor training', in Wilkin, M. (Ed.) (1992a) *Mentoring in schools*. London: Kogan Page, pp.97−115.

Watkins, C. and Whalley, C. (1993) *Mentoring: resources for school-based development*. London: Longman.

Wilkin, M. (1990) 'The development of partnership in the United Kingdom', in Booth, M., Furlong, J. and Wilkin, M. (Eds) (1990) *Partnership in initial teacher training*. London: Cassell, pp.3−23.

Wilkin, M. (Ed.) (1992a), *Mentoring in schools*. London: Kogan Page.

Wilkin, M. (1992b) 'On the cusp: from supervision to mentoring in initial teacher training', *Cambridge Journal of Education*, **22** (1), pp.79−90.

Wilkin, M. and Sankey, D. (Eds) (1994) *Collaboration and transition in initial teacher training*. London: Kogan Page.

Williams, R. (1965) *The long revolution*. Harmondsworth: Pelican.

Winter, R. (1989) 'Teacher appraisal and the development of professional knowledge', in Carr, W. (Ed.) (1989) *Quality teaching: arguments for a reflective profession*. London: Falmer Press, pp.183 – 99.

Wood, P. (1987) 'Life histories and teacher knowledge', in Smyth, J. (Ed.) (1987) *Educating teachers: changing the nature of pedagogical knowledge*. London: Falmer Press, pp.121 – 35.

Wood, P. (1991) 'The cooperating teacher's role in nurturing reflective teaching', in Tabachnick, R. and Zeichner, K. (Eds) (1991) *Issues and practices in inquiry-oriented teacher education*. London: Falmer Press, pp.202 – 10.

Zeichner, K. and Liston, D. (1987) 'Teaching student teachers to reflect', *Harvard Educational Review*, **57** (1), pp.23 – 48.

Index